CLASSIC STEAM

ON SHED

CLASSIC STEAM

ON SHED

A portrait of the steam locomotive depot

David Hucknall

Silver Link Publishing Ltd

First published in December 1993

British Library Cataloguing in Publication Data

A catalogue record for this book is available from the British Library

ISBN 1 85794 012 1

Frontispiece Standing around the turntable at Canklow shed are two typical examples of the depot's allocation of freight locomotives: 'Austerity' Class 2-8-0 No 90030 and an unidentified '8F'. For as long as I could remember Canklow had never cleaned its locomotives particularly well - as long as the number could be read was all that seemed necessary - but by the 1960s there were just too few staff anyway. *D. J. Hucknall*

Silver Link Publishing Ltd
Unit 5
Home Farm Close
Church Street
Wadenhoe
Peterborough PE8 5TE
Tel/fax (0832) 720440

Printed and bound in Great Britain

The directory extracts in Appendix 2 are reproduced from *The British Locomotive Shed Directory* compiled and published by R. S. Grimsley in December 1947.

Opposite The southerly end of Canklow shed, an austere brick-built structure with two parallel pitched roofs. On the left-hand side of the picture is the sandhouse, its standard chimney a design that could be seen from Hellifield to Gloucester. Behind the '8F' is a typical Midland water tank on its brick support. (See also page 41.) *D. J. Hucknall*

Acknowledgements

It gives me very great pleasure to acknowledge those who have helped in some way in the preparation of this book.

I am particularly grateful to Renate McCarron who typed the manuscript with such accuracy and efficiency, and to Chris Silk who dealt with many of the shed logs. I should also like to express my sincere thanks to Mr Derek Mercer who, as usual, printed my difficult negatives so painstakingly, and to Steve Turnbull, whose assistance with shed logs and shed plans was invaluable.

I should like to express my sincere appreciation to Harry Usmar, Alec Swain, Ken Fairey and Roger Duckworth who gave me permission to include some of their excellent photographs in this work. In this context I have reserved my particular thanks to W. A. C. Smith whose superb photographs have contributed so significantly to this book.

Finally, I must acknowledge my own family for their considerable assistance - my wife Susan, who recast my captions when they were particularly tortured, my daughter Rachel, whose eye for a good photograph is infallible, and my son Philip, who made sure I 'stuck at it'.

The Engine Shed Society

The Engine Shed Society is the only association in Britain dedicated solely to the study of motive power depots - both old and new, extinct and extant.

Since its formation in the middle of the last decade, more than 200 members have joined, enabling the society to publish a quality, quarterly illustrated journal, *Link*, and achieve several notable triumphs in the field of preservation. Among the historical buildings members' efforts and representations have so far helped to save from demolition are St Blazey, Staveley Barrow Hill and Peterborough East, while a number of 19th-century steam sheds thought to have long since vanished have been discovered intact!

Modern diesel and electric depots also fall within the ESS remit, as do turntables, coaling plants, workshops and stabling points, etc, and *Link* publishes regular news updates on all aspects of shed life as well as printing photographs (many never previously published) containing a wealth of information for modellers.

An annual meeting is held each autumn - usually at a preserved steam depot. The annual fee if £9 and prospective members should contact John Jarvis, The Laurels, Fire Beacon Lane, Bowd, Sidmouth, Devon EX10 0NE.

Contents

Foreword

Alec Swain
Chairman, The Engine Shed Society

As one who started his railway career as an apprentice fitter in September 1949 and who spent much of his working life from then on within, or associated with, motive power depots, I look forward to a publication which portrays the railways as I knew them in my place of work. To many enthusiasts a depot was just a place where one could see, write down the numbers of and photograph the maximum number of locomotives in the shortest possible time. This was really a pity, as a depot was a fascinating place if one had the time to watch what actually happened - it was not the scene of chaos, with locomotives moving about all over the place, that it sometimes seemed.

The working conditions that had to be endured would just not be tolerated these days. For example, during the re-roofing of each roundhouse in turn at Cricklewood, the shed staff were expected to carry on normally - I can well remember sweeping the snow off a boiler top in a roofless No 1 shed before removing the dome cover for access to the regulator valve within - hoping that the snow would not return before the job was finished. Even if you had the luxury of a roof over your head, the prevailing wind always cut through the buildings like a knife, since they were both through round-houses, and you were grateful for a locomotive on either side of that on which you were working to provide some measure of wind-break.

Then there was always the chance that the inspection pit below your locomotive would be flooded, since the scale and sludge washed out of boilers tended to block the drainage system. This was not an excuse to stop work - you went to the stores and collected a pair of wellington boots (held in stock for that very purpose), which enabled you to wade into the pit and commence work to dismantle the inside valve gear, etc. Naturally you were very careful not to drop the odd nut or cotter pin, or else it was necessary to roll up your sleeve and 'fish' in the somewhat dirty water!

The maintenance of steam locomotives was hard and dirty work, involving shift and weekend working at some-what poor pay, certainly so far as the non-craft trades were concerned. In boom years therefore it became increasingly difficult to recruit, and retain, staff, particularly in the unskilled and labouring grades. There were better-paid jobs with social hours in far more congenial conditions there for the asking, and this was reflected in the unkempt shed yards, particularly around ashpits and coaling plants, where piles of ash and smokebox char accumulated together with spilt coal. Although some depots had mechanical aids to these activities, they still depended on a broom, shovel and wheelbarrow wielded by a human being.

The arrival of immigrant labour from the Commonwealth saved the day in a good many areas, particularly London, and at one depot many of them actually 'lived on the job' and built themselves wooden shacks on the embankment that bordered the shed yard. Gardens and fences soon developed them into small-holdings and, indeed, the milkman called every morning! The management of the day turned a blind eye to all this, being just grateful to find the answer to their labour shortages.

Although the movement of locomotives within the depot may have appeared chaotic to the uninitiated observer, in fact it followed a definite pattern determined in the layout of coaling facilities, ashpits, water columns and sheds, to ensure that after coaling, fire-cleaning and watering, locomotives were stabled in 'time order' for their next job, so avoiding unnecessary movements and perhaps a 'late start' from the shed signal. It was regarded as the top priority of a shedmaster's job to ensure that a suitable locomotive fully prepared for its task ahead was ready at the shed outlet at the diagrammed time as required by the Operating Department, and he had a team of supervisors, footplate staff, fitters, boilersmiths and many other grades behind him.

It should not be forgotten that many depots were long-lived and provided the livelihood and, often, the housing for several generations of railwaymen. Depots and such railway housing estates were communities in themselves and social clubs were encouraged at the larger ones, together with allotment societies and other amenities. A depot of any size had its own (illegal) bookmaker - long before the betting shop came into being - as well as a watchmaker, hairdresser, builder and decorator, etc, who used their hobby skills to provide a much-needed service to their fellow workers and at the same time supplement their income.

Prior to 1948 the railway companies had worked hard to ensure that their employees were happy with their lot (I hesitate to use the modern term 'job satisfaction'), which ensured dedication and loyalty, and this came over very strongly during the formative years of my railway career. Perhaps this book should be dedicated to those who devoted their lives to the steam locomotive, be they footplate men or shed staff of many grades.

Alec Swain is a former Apprentice Fitter and Fitter at Cricklewood MPD, Mechanical Inspector at Manchester Hunts Bank, Mechanical Foreman at Leicester Midland MPD, Diesel Instructor based at Cathays DMU Depot, District Diesel Instructor at Cricklewood Diesel Depot, thereafter a managerial career with modern traction based at Paddington, Reading, BRBHQ Marylebone and Paddington, from where he retired.

Foreword

Eddie Lyons CEng MIStructE
Vice-President, The Engine Shed Society

In our industrial heritage, the steam locomotive has certainly played a significant part. The workhorses of the early 19th century made distribution of goods and public travel an everyday occurrence, while the speed and strength of their successors brought the nation holiday pleasures and great industrial might.

The 'travelling power houses' needed regular attention, care and respect if they were to serve us well . . . hence the development of the locomotive shed.

After the early pioneering days, engine shed activity did not change remarkably. Although locos increased dramatically in size over the years and underwent numerous improvements, they basically retained the same design, their maintenance thereby remaining a highly labour-intensive operation.

The locomotive shed had to cater for the demands of this operation. The larger ones had all to offer, from everyday attention to quite major repairs. The smaller depots generally had the barest of essentials - provision for cover, water, coal and occasionally a turning facility.

Being the major artery for transport for over a hundred years, the railways ran a 24-hour service, therefore requiring a large number of locomotives with their resultant heavy maintenance and upkeep. The companies also had to ensure that sheds were strategically placed on their systems in order to maximise the efficient deployment of passenger and goods workings.

Regardless of shed size and location, however, duties were more or less the same. Crews booked on, read the necessary notices and inspected their allotted engines. Firelighters, cleaners, fitters, boilersmiths and disposal/preparation teams were all part of this hive of activity, whereas at the smaller depots the footplatemen often completed many of these tasks themselves.

There were basically two types of depot: the straight road sheds, with their through or dead-end variations, and the roundhouse types, which although generally square or rectangular were so called because of their covered turntable and radiating roads. All sheds needed a coaling facility. Some of these took the form of a tower, up which coal wagons would be raised and their contents emptied into a hopper above the locomotive coaling line. Others had a ramp approach, coal being literally shovelled out of the wagon into tubs and tipped into the locomotive bunker. Some were merely platforms where the coal was basketed into the engine.

Water towers varied just as much in size, but all served water columns aptly placed in the shed yard. Ash pits, sand bins, turntables, lamp rooms, stores, messrooms, washout points - each had its place. So too, each engine had to be in its rightful place at the right time for each of its maintenance tasks. All this was controlled by clerks, timekeepers and foremen. To the railway enthusiast the large sheds were mysterious, with their offerings of 'away shed' locomotives and all the magic bustle the depot could offer, whereas the smaller sheds had a more romantic atmosphere of tranquillity.

This record of these activities is an excellent reminder of those golden days, of the energy and loyalty given by so many generations of railwaymen.

Eddie Lyons is author of An Historical Survey of Great Western Engine Sheds 1947 *(OPC, 1972) and co-author of* An Historical Survey of Great Western Engine Sheds 1837-1947 *(OPC, 1979).*

Roundhouse interior, Swindon. Out of steam, three tank engines face the turntable: '5700' Class pannier tanks Nos 8779 and 3645 flank '1361' Class No 1364, a Churchward design introduced in 1910 for dock shunting. This locomotive was transferred to Swindon in February 1960 from Plymouth (Laira), and when this photograph was taken was still displaying an 83D shed plate. The '1361ST' was withdrawn in January 1961. No 8779 was withdrawn in February 1962, while No 3645 survived three months longer. *D. J. Hucknall collection*

Introduction

I have only a vague recollection of my first sight of a large engine shed. I cannot remember where or when, apart from the fact that it was very early on a summer Saturday and we were on our annual holiday, travelling from Sheffield to Devon on an overnight train. The shed may have been Bristol Bath Road, seen through the tired eyes of a small boy on a misty morning, but, like a single snap in an album, I can still see a line of green-grey locomotives above brown and silver rails. My parents tell me that everyone in the compartment collected numbers for me. Needless to say, the list was lost.

My first real opportunity to get to grips with engine sheds came in the summer of 1952, when my parents gave me a Rudge bicycle. It was no problem at all to get to Canklow, Grimethorpe, Mexborough and Doncaster. At the time, however, I and my contemporaries were not particularly interested in some of them. Canklow and Mexborough had nothing that we could not see day after day at Parkgate & Rawmarsh or Parkgate & Aldwarke stations. Our abiding passion was for the Heaton 'Pacifics', coming out through the latter station on the Newcastle-Bournemouth trains in the morning and returning in the evening - engines such as *Book Law*, *Dick Turpin* and *Velocity*. We would linger until dusk for a glimpse of the Kingmoor and Corkerhill engines - *Ocean*, *Sanspareil* and *Revenge* - that dashed through on freights between Carlisle and Leicester.

Doncaster was another matter. It attracted us like a magnet but had a reputation for impregnability. We used to sit on the wooden fence and watch the traffic to and from the coaler but there was no question of entering the shed proper. Of equal interest was the 'Plant'. This was surrounded by a high red-brick wall, but we knew a place where you could peer over if you stood on the saddle of your bike and steadied yourself against a handy gas-lamp. This gave us a view through the grimy windows of the paint shop. That shadowy shape, covered in patches of pink primer, was surely *Sir Visto* from Carlisle Canal shed!

Over the years how many casual conversations have unexpectedly revealed a fellow devotee of engine sheds! Wistful reminiscences have disclosed that there was, in fact, an unofficial route into Crewe North shed, over the wall or the fence off Lockitt Street. (The only route I ever used was the official one over the footbridge at the end of the platform.) A respectable professional man sheepishly admitted 'Longsight was the only shed I was ever thrown out of'. I have been reliably informed that, with certain sheds, if you appeared in school cap and blazer and began the conversation with 'Excuse me, Sir,' you would not only be admitted to the shed but also have a guide.

When I went to Edinburgh to work in the 1960s, St Margarets was a relatively short distance from where I was living. The nearness of a shed of such a size and history fired my enthusiasm, especially as I now had a reliable camera and an excellent exposure meter. I would also seize any available opportunity to visit other sheds in Scotland. My first chance to visit Perth depot came in August 1964, when I persuaded my landlady to include me in a party of Church of Scotland ladies on an outing from Leith. I even asked the driver to drop me off and pick me up outside 63A.

The Scottish sheds, even in the mid-1960s, refreshed my jaded English palate. The locomotives were tolerably clean and sometimes appeared fresh from the works at Cowlairs or Inverurie. Happily they were too far away from the growing band of so-called 'enthusiasts' who were appearing in English sheds at this time, armed with tool kits and prepared to remove anything of value from locomotives.

Because my unofficial requests to 'take a few photographs' were never refused, I always tried to take them without interfering with the work of the shed staff. I assumed that they were too busy and that their work was too important to have me pestering them with trivial questions.

To me, everything about a locomotive seemed either extremely hot or extremely cold. The sheer weight and size of the tools needed to maintain or clean the fires were quite daunting. Ashpit work, particularly, must have been absolute drudgery - standing under the locomotive, pulling out lumps of hot clinker through the ashpan for long periods, surrounded by corrosive fumes. I clearly remember one man at 64A who regularly emptied the smokeboxes. His overalls were soaked in sweat. I saw his hand, resting on a standpipe, hard, horny and burned. Some depots had mechanical coalers, but in many, men filled tubs and man-handled them to chutes over the tender. On the whole of the Western Region, for example, only three sheds had mechanical coalers.

As I compiled the photographs for this book, it brought home to me the massive under-investment in the railway system that had taken place over many years. Lack of maintenance during the war was never made good. Facilities and equipment, even at large sheds, deteriorated further and further. Work on steam locomotives, already so dirty and laborious, was made harder by an acute shortage of labour. It remains a lasting tribute to the dedication of the staff over the years that locomotives capable of fulfilling arduous schedules continued to emerge from our steam depots.

Right The entrance to 64A was off Clockmill Road and led into a passage on the left-hand side of which were glass-fronted, illuminated notice-boards. A driver would spend ten or so minutes checking these to see whether any restrictions had arisen on the route since he had signed for his 'notice'. Other boards gave diagram numbers against which were the numbers of the locomotives picked to work them.

From the end of the passage one could look across the lines to the coal stage and the shed. Behind, the sooted sandstone tenements on London Road loomed. When I knew St Margarets it was a mere shadow of its former self as far as its allocation of locomotives was concerned. It had once had a very large allocation of undistinguished engines, and it is hard to imagine what working then in the place would have been like. Charles Meacher, who had worked there, wrote, 'It was always a dismal environment but on a Sunday night, when the engines had just been kindled, the cold boilers and black reek made it even more depressing.' *D. J. Hucknall*

Below No one who has ever lived close to the East Coast Main Line will forget the chime whistle of the 'A4s' - there was a haunting quality about it made even more poignant by a misty day. On such a day, No 60026 *Miles Beevor* stands, fully coaled and awaiting further duties, on St Margarets, against a backdrop of the 300-foot-long coaling stage and the tenements of Edinburgh. Soon, after a brief note on that wonderful whistle, she will move off shed with that unmistakeable sound of a large Gresley engine - a panting sizzle coming from her chimney and the characteristic ringing from her motion. *D. J. Hucknall*

1. Disposal

Ash, clinker and smokebox char appeared to cover every square inch of the ground in and around an engine shed. From the cinder path to the boundary fences, it was underfoot and often in heaps. In forgotten or abandoned areas it even provided sustenance for clumps of rosebay willowherb and toadflax. Battered wheelbarrows being filled by stooping men scraping and shovelling by the side of almost buried tracks was a sight repeated throughout our railway system in the days of steam. From Okehampton to Kettering and from Stewarts Lane to St Margarets, men were engaged in a seemingly endless struggle to control it.

Coaling, watering and fire-cleaning were the immediate tasks to be undertaken when a locomotive arrived on shed after duty. Engines could come on to the ash roads with fires so clinkered that it would require hours of back-breaking pushing and heaving with shovel and dart, in front of a fire radiating enough heat to sear the skin. The tools were soon red hot and soft enough to be useless. I recall reading about an 'ROD' on the Western Region that came on to a shed with a fire that took a shift and a half to remove.

Underneath the engine, the dampers would be opened wide and ash would be pushed and pulled from the ashpan with the rake. As it cascaded from the pan, clouds of dust would be whirled by unpredictable draughts and winds through the motion and wheels to cover the poor fire-cleaner.

I remember seeing No 60100 at 64A on the track next to the gulley wreathed in dense clouds of white vapour (probably dilute sulphuric acid if the truth were known). Charles Meacher (in *LNER Footplate Memories*, D.

Bradford Barton) comments, 'It hardly seems possible that human beings could survive in such conditions'. He goes on to describe the well-worn path between the ash lyes at 64A and the pub ('Jock's Lodge') used for regular visits to wash away the fumes.

Some sheds (for example York, Leicester and Crewe) had fairly elaborate ash disposal systems. York had a wet ashpit with grills like a cattle-grid where men could walk while allowing the removed ash and clinker to fall into a water-filled pit below. Others, such as St Margarets, had a pit-side slaking hydrant and dumped ashes were doused under and by the side of the locomotive. Whereas York had a crane with a grab to shift the ashes from the pit, 64A had men with shovels and wagons in the gulley.

Smokebox cleaning was the last of the really unpleasant jobs. Depending on the state of the fire and the nature of the fuel, the amount of ash in the smokebox could vary immensely. Sometimes there were no problems. On other occasions, however, the char would be ready to pour out of the door over the bicycle-clipped trousers and boots of the disposal man, over the buffer beam and on to the track. A fine abrasive material that could find its way into the motion as well as the clothing of the fire-dropper, it had to be dug out and thrown well down-wind of the engine. Afterwards, the door sealing face had to be cleaned, the very heavy smokebox door had to be shut, and the running-plate swept. E. S. Beevor (in *Steam Motive Power Depots*, Ian Allan 1983) says that a fair impression of a shed could be formed from the state of the ashpits. He comments, 'If they were constantly piled up with ashes, then there were not enough shed men or the management was indifferent - or both.'

Above This photograph, taken at Lostock Hall shed near Preston, shows two engines - ex-L&YR Aspinall '3F' No 12317 and another 'Austerity' - approaching the 'No 2' coaler, built in 1937. In 1938 the vacuum-operated turntable in the foreground was installed. In the centre and on the right-hand side of the photograph can be seen the gas lamps, with their permanently positioned metal ladders, that lit the yard. The cleanliness of the lamp glass, although essential, is surprising given the general atmosphere around an engine shed. *R. G. Duckworth*

Left Here at Canklow shed, Rotherham, in April 1964, 18 months before the shed was closed, we see wagons full of locomotive coal lined up ready for use on the coaling stage.

'Austerity' No 90153 and 'B1' No 61327 are typical of the type (and condition) of the engines associated with the shed in its later years. No 90153 had been part of a batch of 150 2-8-0 locomotives built in 1943/44 by the North British Loco Co for use overseas by the British Army. The 'Austerities' were remarkably ugly engines - the chimney was squat (at just over 9 inches high), the coupled wheels were small (a diameter of only 4 ft 8½ in), and the smoke-box diameter was significantly less than that of the boiler clothing plate. *D. J. Hucknall*

Right The track in the foreground at Lostock Hall shed used to lead to one of the large stacks where a considerable amount of coal was stored in earlier years. Fowler LMS '7F' 0-8-0 No 9595 (probably allocated to Aintree shed at the time) is seen some time in the late 1940s. Behind it, partially hidden by the row of water columns, stands an 'Austerity' 2-8-0, the type of engine that eventually replaced the 0-8-0s, over 100 of the latter being scrapped between 1949 and 1951. *R. G. Duckworth*

Above A battered mineral wagon, two Perth 'Black Fives' and Kingmoor's 'Britannia' No 70010 (formerly *Owen Glendower*) stabled in the yard at Perth in June 1965. The background is dominated by the 'No 1'-type coaling plant that had been built on the site of the old engine shed of the Scottish Central Railway (a constituent company of the Caledonian Railway).

LMS coaling plants are well-described by Hawkins and Reeve (in *LMS Engine Sheds*, Vol 1 The LNWR). Essentially they contained 300 tons of coal divided between two equal hoppers filled using 20-ton containers loaded from railway wagons using a tippler. Even from a distance fascinating details can be seen - the large pair of counterweights on the front outer wall to balance the containers, the wagon tippler on the lower left-hand side and the pair of chutes with jigger motors, each serving one road. *D. J. Hucknall*

Left Another Kingmoor 'Britannia' No 70008 (formerly *Black Prince*) is seen under the coaler on the evening of Friday 25 June 1965.

In operation, coal from the hopper was fed on to an oscillating metal plate and, falling over the edge, fell into a chute and was deflected into the tender. The control hut (strong enough to withstand the impact of large lumps of coal) contained the chute-angle controls and water valves for a sprinkler system to lay the coal dust. *D. J. Hucknall*

Above Stirling's locomotive allocation in 1965 consisted on nine 'Black Fives', and one of them, No 45084, is seen by the coaler at St Margarets shed, Edinburgh (64A), on the afternoon of 17 April 1965. The afternoon was dreary, the engine dirty and with the 'black hole' of the coaler forming the backdrop, the subject was horribly unpromising. Nevertheless, it was worth attempting because it was the one and only occasion I saw a Stirling engine at 64A. *D. J. Hucknall*

Right The disposal crew at St Margaret's set the road for 'A4' Class No 60026 *Miles Beevor* on a drizzly Saturday afternoon in March 1965. Behind the locomotive is a slightly clearer view of the coal bank, where the coalmen filled half-ton tubs by hand and then man-handled them into position over a waiting tender.

By 1965 No 60026 was rather dilapidated, but it had been a King's Cross engine in the heyday of the steam-hauled Anglo-Scottish expresses on the East Coast Main Line and performed with distinction. On 6 November 1956, for example, it was hauling the down 'Talisman', which had left London 23 minutes late. It was driven by Bill Hoole, one of a group of drivers whose exploits were lauded by the railway journals of the 1950s. In a brilliant run not only was the whole loss recovered by Durham, but also arrival in Newcastle was 6 minutes early. *D. J. Hucknall*

'A1' Class 4-6-2 No 60131 *Osprey* at Carlisle Kingmoor a few months before its withdrawal in 1965. Dominating the background is the No 1-type coaler that figures so prominently in this and other photographs of Kingmoor. With tongue in cheek, Hawkins and Reeve (*LMS Engine Sheds*, Vol 5) pointed out that once the engines they had served had gone, these massive concrete structures were 'outstandingly useless', deemed an insurance risk by the authorities and 'liable to collapse if a trespassing child bounced its ball on the side'.

Osprey was a Copley Hill (37B) engine in the 1950s, and while there the locomotive and its crews put in months of splendid work on duties such as the 'Queen of Scots'. In 1954, for example, 60131 appeared every day between 13 and 26 June on either the 'West Riding' or the 'Yorkshire Pullman', and was regularly 'mentioned in dispatches'. One of C. J. Allen's correspondents (*Trains Illustrated*, October 1956) reported a run behind No 60131 on the 5.3 pm Newcastle to King's Cross during which, with 10 coaches, it reached 96 mph near Essendine and averaged almost 88 mph over the 15.2 miles from Corby Glen to Helpston. From July 1963 *Osprey* was transferred to Leeds Neville Hill shed (together with Nos 60118 and 60134) and was often borrowed by Holbeck for various duties. No 60131 was no stranger to Carlisle. For example, on Saturday 1 August 1964 it brought in the 09.05 Leeds-Glasgow (St Enoch). Two weeks later it reappeared with a down relief to the 'Thames-Clyde Express'. *D. J. Hucknall*

Above The coaling plant also dominates this 1965 scene at Kingmoor. On a miserable March day in 1965 a dirty 'Black Five', No 45092, and a neglected 'Clan' 'Pacific', No 72009 (formerly *Clan Stewart*) stand amidst a confusion of oil drums and locomotive kindling.

No 72009 was completed in the spring of 1952 and stationed at Kingmoor, one of five such locomotives. Before the depot received 'Coronation' Class 'Pacifics', one of the duties of the 'Clans' involved working the 9.50 am Euston to Perth forward from Carlisle. In September 1958 No 72009 was tried out on the Clacton line of the Eastern Region. It was hoped that five 'Clans' could be exchanged for five 'Britannias', which would have gone to Holbeck. However, No 72009 was regarded as 'little better than a good B1'. *D. J. Hucknall*

Right A group of railwaymen and trainspotters stand with Class 'A2' 4-6-2 No 60532 *Blue Peter* at Kingmoor in October 1966. *Blue Peter* had worked a Special Excursion pulled by the last remaining 'A2' 'Pacific' from Edinburgh (fare 35 shillings) via the Waverley route (outward) and Beattock (return). Unusually, the train ran complete with passengers from Citadel station to Kingmoor so that they could visit the shed. *W. A. C. Smith*

'V2' 2-6-2 No 60963 at York shed, its home depot, under the huge 500-ton coaling stage built there in 1932. Close examination reveals the coaler to be in a poor state.

In an attempt to improve their steaming characteristics following a deterioration in the quality of the coal supplied, two 'V2s', Nos 60963 (built in January 1943, original number 3675) and 60817, were fitted with double blastpipes and double chimneys of the 'Royal Scot' type without Kylchap cowls. It was concluded, however, that there was 'no dramatic improvement in steaming' (see *Locomotives of the LNER, Part 6C*, RCTS 1984). *D. J. Hucknall*

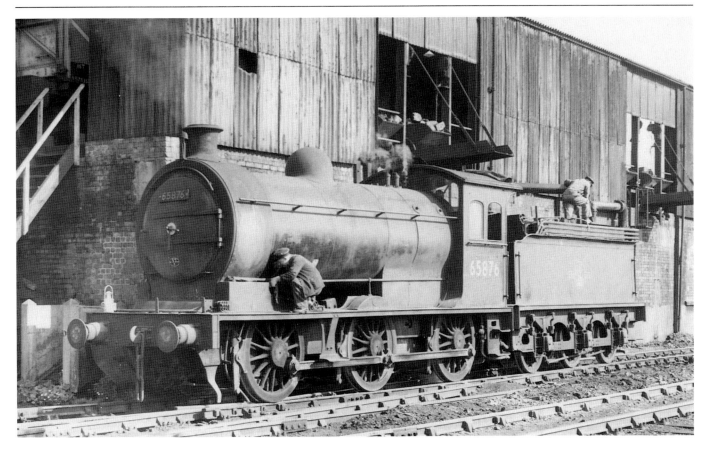

Above South Blyth shed, Northumberland, on 19 September 1963 - 'J27' No 65876 is being prepared for yet another round of short hauls from pit to port and back. As she stands by the coaling stage one of the crew supervises the watering while the other lubricates the inside gear. Above the locomotive's tender is the coaling chute with tubs containing substantial lumps of coal awaiting discharge. *K. C. H. Fairey*

Below Stanier 2-6-0 No 42959 (5B) at Springs Branch depot, Wigan, stand-ing in front of the shed's rather odd-looking coaler on 24 September 1961.

In the course of my trainspotting days on the Midland Region line between Rotherham and Leeds, I suppose I saw just a couple of Stanier's 2-6-0s. This was hardly surprising - they were allocated to sheds such as Crewe (North and South), Aston, Preston and Birkenhead. Introduced in 1933, there were 40 locomotives in the Class. I was very surprised to find that they had a power classification '6P5F' and, nominally, a tractive effort (26,290 lb) that exceeded that of a 'Black Five'. *K. C. H. Fairey*

'County' Class 4-6-0 No 1004 *County of Somerset* is seen here by Penzance's coal stage, a typical GWR brick structure with, once again, a water tank forming the roof. Inside the stage can be seen a metal mineral wagon containing coal that was discharged on to the metal floor at coaling level and then loaded into tubs. No 1004 was built in 1945. From December 1960 until its withdrawal in September 1962 it was allocated to Penzance mpd. *H. G. Usmar*

Right The preserved coaling stage at Didcot, although beginning to show its 60 years of age, remains virtually unchanged from the days of the GWR in this recent view. Forty-three feet wide, the entire roof consists of a water tank (74,320 gallons capacity). The two coal tips are obscured by 'Hall' No 6998 *Burton Agnes Hall* as she passes by to take up her duties. The letters 'CDF' close up to the buffer beam of the locomotive are the GWR coding for Cardiff (Canton) depot, to which shed the engine had once been allocated. *D. J. Hucknall*

Below At Brighton shed on 23 June 1956 'L' Class 4-4-0 No 31776 is having its 4-ton tender coaled to capacity by a crane-held hopper.

The 'L1s' had been designed for the South Eastern & Chatham Railway by H. S. Wainwright and his Chief Draughtsman. When R. E. L. Maunsell joined the SECR as CME, he modified the existing drawings and then had 22 locomotives built - 12 by Beyer Peacock and Co Ltd and 10 by A. Borsig in Berlin; the Borsig engines arrived in England in May 1914. When new the engines were allocated to Bricklayers Arms, Cannon Street, Dover and Hastings. May 1949 found them at Tonbridge, Ashford, Stewarts Lane, Ramsgate and St Leonards. In early 1956 Nos 31776/77 and 78 went to Brighton, working to Tonbridge, Bournemouth and Salisbury. *W. A. C. Smith*

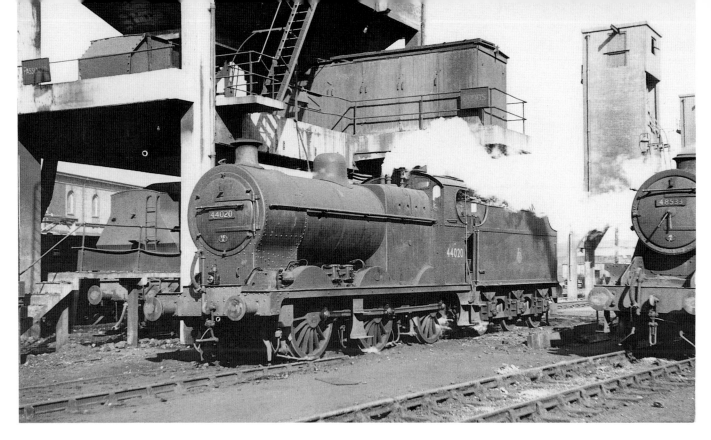

Above Wellingborough '4F' Class 0-6-0 No 44020 stands under the coaler at Leicester Midland shed (15C) on 3 March 1961. Above the cab of the '4F' the board on the railings reads 'GOODS' - the other road under the coaler is designated 'PASSENGER'. Different grades of coal were available at depots covering both types of duty and the goods engines were given the poorer grades. The running foreman had to keep his eyes open for the driver who tried to top up his locomotive's tender with better coal by nipping under the passenger bunker.

To the left-hand side of the '4F', in the road leading to and from the ash-pit, stands Staveley '8F' No 48533. *A. Swain*

Below Another view of the coal and ash plants at Leicester Midland shed. On 25 March 1961 No 61138 (41D), obviously recently ex-works, looks superb with her lined-out black livery as she simmers in the spring sunshine.

As the influence of the Eastern Region gradually increased in the former Midland territory, so its engines began to be seen in areas and on trains which had never been their responsibility. On 25 July 1958, for example, 'B1' Class No 61136 (Neasden, 14D) appeared on a regular train (the 8.52 am Bradford-St Pancras) for the first time since the 1948 Exchanges; it was piloting 'Jubilee' No 45627 *Sierra Leone*. By 1959/60 the 'B1s' were travelling up the Midland main line to London. Canklow's 'B1s' Nos 61312/34 were alternating on the 2.28 am Class 'B' Masboro-St Pancras and the 11.15 pm Class 'C' from St Pancras to Leicester in the first week or so of 1960. Later that year the 'B1s' had a weekend local diagram covering Nottingham, Leicester and Kettering. *A. Swain*

Watering the newly arrived locomotive was another disposal task. I photographed 'B1' Class No 61278 at Dundee (Tay Bridge) station on a raw day in March 1965. The sharp silhouette of the typical North British Railway water column shows the small stove strapped to the base to prevent the water freezing in cold weather. As the water is taken on the fireman attends to his varied duties, which would include climbing on the tender to put the 'bag' in position, bringing the coal forward and generally trimming the tender so that everything was secure and no lumps would fall off and cause injury. *D. J. Hucknall*

Left Originally there were 40 NBR Class 'D' (LNER Class 'J83') 0-6-0 tank engines, and with the exception of No 8462 the Class was intact on the formation of British Railways. They were very useful engines indeed and, apart from the three shedded at Kipps, all covered at least a million miles each.

Here No 68479 (built by Sharp, Stewart and Co in May 1901) is being watered at Eastfield depot, Glasgow, on 25 August 1958. Eastfield's 'J83s' shunted at Cadder and Maryhill yards and assisted with banking on Cowlairs incline. For this duty No 68479 was fitted with a slip coupling, and the pulley and activating wire can clearly be seen.

The introduction of increasing numbers of diesel shunters brought about the gradual withdrawal of the Class, and No 68479 was one of a group withdrawn in October 1962. The last of the class (No 68477) finally departed two months later. *K. C. H. Fairey*

Right With sleeves rolled up and jackets abandoned, the crew of '5600' Class 0-6-2T No 6613 prepare to water the locomotive at Neath (Court Sart) shed on 24 June 1958. Water at the depot was pumped from a well fed from the Neath canal and stored in tanks over the coal stage.

Court Sart had two subsheds (Neath N&B and Glyn Neath), and provided locomotives for main-line work, shunting, banking and freight services on the Vale of Neath. In mid-1953 the shed staff included 110 drivers, 105 firemen, 21 cleaners, 38 shed grades, 26 fitters (and fitters' mates) and four boilersmiths and their mates. *K. C. H. Fairey*

Left Water spills across '9400' Class No 8481 and tumbles away as her tank is overfilled at Old Oak Common depot (81A) on 8 March 1964. The strengthening sun casts the shadow of the water column sharply across the boiler of 'Castle' Class No 4082 *Windsor Castle*.

No 8481 was a latecomer to 81A, arriving in February 1963 from the Welsh valleys where she had served at Radyr and Barry. By March 1965 Old Oak Common was closed to steam, and No 8481 was withdrawn in June of the same year. *K. C. H. Fairey*

Dominating this photograph is a former Midland Railway swan-neck water column at Canklow shed; behind it, 'B1' Class 4-6-0 No 61394 stands over an ashpit. Scattered on the ground are various tools for fire-cleaning, including long and short shovels. In the lower left-hand corner of the picture and behind the bag of the water column is what appears to be a 'Western Dart', essential a 12-foot long chisel developed on the GWR, which could be used for really badly clinkered grates. In front of the 'Black Five' stands a wagon completely full of ash and clinker awaiting disposal. *D. J. Hucknall*

Left The dirty and unpleasant job of clearing ash from the smokebox of No 7800 *Torquay Manor* is performed by one of the disposal crew at Aberystwyth depot on 30 May 1964. No 7800 had worked a special for the Gainsborough Model Railway Society from Oswestry to Aberystwyth via Moat Lane Junction and Machynlleth, and a great deal of ash would have been produced during the climb to Talerddig (9 miles at 1 in 71 and 1 in 211). The return journey was worse, however. After an easy road from Machynlleth to Cemmes Road, the climb to Talerddig was formidable (8½ miles at 1 in 90, 1 in 60 and 1 in 52). *D. J. Hucknall*

Below One of the disposal crew at Canklow shed is shown clearing char from the smokebox of 'B1' Class 4-6-0 No 61394 on 22 May 1965. This uncomfortable and dirty task was made worse in windy weather, and the noise from the blower jet could be particularly unpleasant. The joint faces had then to be wiped clean and the very heavy smokebox door closed.

Behind the 'B1' is 'Black Five' No 45118 (formerly of 12A and 26A), buffered up to the ever-present wagons full of ash and clinker. Although the crews had no complaints whatsoever about either, boilersmiths apparently preferred the 'B1s' on washout. *D. J. Hucknall*

Right Only a few years before, 'Black Five' No 45118 would have been an extraordinary visitor to Canklow. A clue can be seen in the remnants of the tablet-catching apparatus on the cab side - up until late June 1963, when she went to Newton Heath, she had been a Carlisle (Kingmoor) engine. Then her only visits to Rotherham would have been on one of the express freight trains such as the Buchanan Street-St Pancras that ran over the North Midland route late in the night. *D. J. Hucknall*

Below A schoolboy's view of locomotives at Banbury mpd on the afternoon of 6 August 1958. Looking towards the east across the overgrown sidings and the forgotten piles of clinker, a group of locomotives can be seen behind the elevated road leading to the coaler. In the background is what remains of one of the shed's ash-dropping shelters.

It was obviously the 'Hall', No 4978 *Westwood Hall*, a visitor from Taunton, that had caught my attention, but on either side could be seen a '43XX' Class 2-6-0 and a '2551' Class 0-6-0. At the beginning of her career, in the summer of 1932, No 4978 was a Truro engine, but soon afterwards she moved, eventually finding her way to Taunton. *D. J. Hucknall*

Left Photographed against the background of the repair shop, 'V2' Class 2-6-2 No 60824 stands at St Margarets. The shed was singularly lacking in refinement, and had no ash-handling plant to assist the locomotive disposal crew. In the foreground is one of the ash disposal roads and just visible in the bottom left-hand corner of the photograph are wagons into which the ash and clinker had to be shovelled. Red-hot clinker was doused with water from the stand-pipe on the left. Labouring on the ash-road was hard and unpleasant. Clouds of dust and acrid vapour were produced when the clinker was wetted - the fumes dried the throat, burned the eyes and left a metallic, bitter taste in the mouth. Sweat-soaked overalls and boots lasted half as long as normal under these conditions.

No 60824 (Dec 1937 to Sept 1966; original number 4795) was sent (together with Nos 4796/98) to St Margarets in October 1945 from Doncaster. It is interesting to recall that on 19 September 1955, for the first time on record, an ex-LNER engine (actually No 60824) hauled the 3.30 pm 'Postal' out of Aberdeen. *D. J. Hucknall*

Right Moving away from the ashpit at 64A is Standard Class '4' 2-6-4T No 80055, while sister engine No 80022 is still receiving attention. When over a pit the disposal fireman could get under the locomotive to rake out the ashpan; the disposal crew could also ladle out clinker and ash through the firebox door and throw it out on the side of the pit. In the siding adjacent to No 80022 there is a line of wagons below ground level which received the debris from fire cleaning and dropping. *D. J. Hucknall*

Left Another view of the fire-cleaning road at St Margarets. Ash and clinker would be ladled out of the firebox by a toiling fireman, the shovel and fire irons getting hotter and hotter the longer the fire took to clear. Years before, with a line of waiting engines, the process would have illuminated the night as cascades of red-hot debris hit the pit side and the glare from the open firebox lit up the sweating faces of the crews. By the side of the locomotives, piles of clinker would glow, ticking and pinging as it cooled.

These pictures can only hint at the primitive conditions, but a discarded, bent rake, a pile of ash steaming in the drizzle, and rusting mineral wagons already full can still evoke the memory of this laborious and sometimes painful job. *D. J. Hucknall*

Above BR Standard Class '5' No 73000 (41D) is ready to run on to the ashpit at Leicester Midland shed on 8 March 1961. In the background, to the right of the locomotive's tender and already glimpsed in the pictures on page 20, can be seen the shed's concrete ashplants. Ashes were either thrown out of the firebox from the footplate and into tubs alongside, or discharged from the ashpan into similar containers beneath the loco. The tubs could be emptied through their bottoms and the ash fell into a sloping, lined channel with a skip at its lowest point. When full, the skip was raised along guide rails by an electric hoist located at the top of the plant. As it neared the top the skip was tilted and the contents fell down into waiting wagons. A few years before, No 73000 and her sister No 73001 double-headed an experimental fully-fitted coal train between Toton and Brent as part of an investigation into the possibility of equipping all freight vehicles with a continuous braking system. *A. Swain*

Right 'Black Five' No 45461 stands by the ash-lifting plant at Perth shed in 1965. Some of the tools required for fire cleaning can be seen propped up against the tender and lying on the ground. Before the fire could be cleaned, the front and rear compartments of the ashpan had to be cleaned. An ashpan rake was about 15 feet long and the front of the ashpan was dealt with by manhandling the rake through a gap in the firebars and ramming it hard in the direction of the front damper. The rear ashpan could be cleaned using a curved engine rake while standing on the track below the cab. *D. J. Hucknall*

2. Turntables

When a locomotive arrived on shed, the disposal crew were told by the foreman whether or not it should be turned and where it should be stabled. Some sheds had a triangle on which an engine could be turned, but the majority had one or more turntables.

The inconvenience that an out-of-action turntable could cause was immense. In the early spring of 1953, for example, Perth's turntable was replaced. The work took six weeks and during that time some extraordinary manoeuvres were necessary. For instance, the 5A 'Pacific' off the 7.20 pm from Euston travelled to Dundee to turn. Similarly, at the end of May 1956 Penzance's turntable was under repair, and to avoid tender-first working, tender engines were serviced and turned at Truro shed. Several 2-6-2Ts were temporarily drafted to 83F for the workings between Truro and Penzance.

Even by the late 19th century many depots in Britain had been in existence for a very long time. They could be, in some cases, appallingly inefficient. A distorted or corroded turntable, invariably manually operated, could disrupt the work of a depot during breakdowns or after accidents.

During the 1930s companies such as the LMS set in motion ambitious modernisation schemes, which included turntable replacement. The manual turntables were removed, and larger, vacuum-operated machines were installed at over 100 depots. Turntables to the Mundt or Vogele design were in most cases supplied by Cowans Sheldon or Ransome & Rapier. Even this essential work was piecemeal and badly co-ordinated. As Hawkins, Hooper and Reeve (in *British Railways Engine Sheds, London Midland Matters*, Irwell Press 1989) amusingly recall, 'Rather like the successive Gas Board/Electricity Board excavations of our roads, the turntable boys would arrive separately and the roofing firm would turn up months (or years) before or after. . .'.

Even immediately before the end of steam, turntable replacement was thought necessary, some fortunate sheds getting electric systems that were wonderfully easy to control. Elsewhere men struggled to the end, pushing carefully balanced locomotives round hopelessly inadequate 'tables.

In the end, however, it was all for nothing. Diesel locomotives rendered turntables redundant, and this essential feature of steam shed activity rapidly disappeared.

What wonderful photographs could have been taken from the flats to the rear of this turntable! Appearing to be almost under their balconies, rebuilt 'West Country' Class No 34018 *Axminster* is turned at Nine Elms on 4 September 1965. No 34018 was one of the Bulleid 'Pacifics' modified according to designs prepared at Brighton under the direction of W. J. A. Sykes (then the CME of the Southern Region), and the result was a handsome, well-proportioned locomotive.

If the locomotive was being prepared for a run it would, after turning, be taken by the preparation crew down to the coaling plant to top up the tender. The relevant headcode would be put up and the engine run forward to await signals to cross the main line and then reverse to Waterloo.
A. Swain

Above Standing on the outside turntable at Leicester Midland shed on 3 March 1961 is unrebuilt 'Patriot' Class 4-6-0 No 45537 *Private E. Sykes V.C.* (then shedded at Nuneaton, 2B). It had worked the daily pick-up freight from Nuneaton and would be returned in the same way.

The 'Patriots' were introduced in 1933 but were overwhelmed by the large numbers of 'Jubilees' that began to be introduced one year later and gradually they were relegated to fitted freight and stopping passenger trains. In 1950 No 45537 had been one of six 'Patriots' allocated to Preston for working Blackpool expresses. Transferred to Rugby (2A), she was then one of four sisters (Nos 45533/37/41/48) to be moved on from there to Nuneaton in January 1961. The unrebuilt 'Patriots' were, in my opinion,

well-proportioned engines. Occasionally they worked on the Midland main line on expresses between Bradford and St Pancras (for example, No 45520 on 4 January 1956; No 45539 on 19 June 1954). Indeed, the last one of the Class I remember seeing was at Roundwood near Rotherham when No 45511 *Isle of Man*, magnificently clean, was working an up Bradford train. *A. Swain*

Below Another view of No 45537. To the left of the locomotive is a stored '2P' 4-4-0, No 40543. Leicester shed closed to steam on 13 June 1966, but the repair shop containing the wheeldrop, seen behind the '2P', continued to survive into the 1970s. *A. Swain*

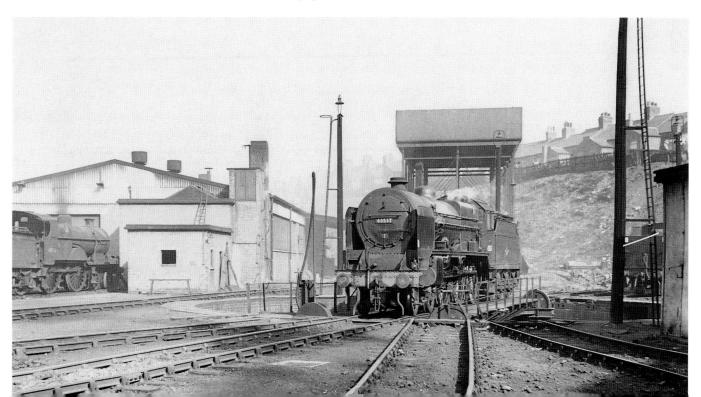

Above 'Hall' No 4935 *Ketley Hall*, then allocated to Didcot (81E), is seen on the 70-foot turntable at Crewe South (5B) on 15 May 1954. 'Halls' were not a particularly unusual sight at Crewe. In the mid-1950s there were two regular workings of WR tender engines into Crewe station, and one usually involved an 84A 'Hall'. Exeter shed had a regular working through to Crewe on freights in the late 1950s (for example, No 4948 *Northwick Hall* on 25 October 1958 and No 4944 *Middleton Hall* on 15 November 1958).

To the rear of the 'Hall' can be seen 5B's coaling plant. According to Hawkins and Reeve, it had been built by the LNWR in 1920 and subsequently modified by the LMS by the incorporation of a wagon hoist. *W. A. C. Smith*

Below On 1 June 1963 the Scottish Locomotive Society organised a special train named 'The Jacobite', booked as 'the last train on the West Highland line'. It was plagued with problems. It left Glasgow double-headed by No 256 *Glen Douglas* and 'J37' No 64632. At Gorton, 8½ miles from Bridge of Orchy, No 64632 failed and No 256 took the train to Rannoch where a pilot locomotive (No D6137) assisted to Fort William. Two other 'J37s', Nos 64592 and 64636, then took the train on to Mallaig. Further problems arose when the brick arch on No 256 collapsed and No 64592 ran hot at Mallaig. A diesel locomotive was used to haul the train on the entire return journey.

In this photograph No 64592, coaled to capacity with high-quality fuel, is seen being turned at Mallaig. This was a subshed of Fort William and occupied a site overlooking the sea. *W. A. C. Smith*

Above On the turntable inside what had been the Highland Railway's semi-roundhouse at Inverness is Class 'K2/2' 2-6-0 No 61792 of Keith shed. Behind its tender can be seen the impressive stone archway through which locomotives entered the shed; it concealed a 45,000-gallon water tank.

The 'K2/2' Class were unpopular and elderly engines introduced in 1914, but only arriving in the North East of Scotland in 1952-3. Keith's 'K2s' were often relegated to freight work, but when this picture was taken on 25 August 1959, No 61792 was booked to work the 12.45 pm Inverness-Aberdeen passenger train as far as Elgin. *W. A. C. Smith*

Below The 'K2' Class were long associated with the West Highland Line, a route with formidable gradients. The last working of the Class took placed on 17 June 1961 when, at the request of Mr W. A. C. Smith, 'K2' No 61764 *Loch Arkaig* hauled the 2.50 pm (Saturdays only) Glasgow (Queen Street)-Crianlarich Upper and the 8.10 pm return. Crianlarich lay 8½ miles from Ardlui and was reached by an arduous climb, most at 1 in 60, up Glen Falloch. This photograph, taken at the time, shows *Loch Arkaig* being turned outside the former locomotive shed at Crianlarich. In the shed (which still stands) were a Wickham PW trolley and stored 'D11' Class No 62688 *Ellen Douglas*. *W. A. C. Smith*

Above Gresley Class 'V1' 2-6-2T No 67610 stands on the turntable at Haymarket shed, Edinburgh, on 19 August 1960. The fully lined if rather dirty black livery, the smokebox-door step, the 1923-type 1 ft 4 in chimney (a very slightly narrower version was fitted to the 'O2s' and 'B1s') and the railed coal bunker are sharply shown. As LNER No 2910, No 67610 had been built in 1931 in Doncaster and sent to Haymarket to work the suburban services around Edinburgh. The 'V1s' also worked to Corstorphine and Gorebridge and hauled stopping trains to Larbert and Caldercruix. As the diesel multiple units appeared, so the 'V1s' and 'V3s' gradually disappeared. No 67610 was withdrawn in June 1961. *K. C. H. Fairey*

Below The tremendous effort required to turn 61 tons of locomotive manually can be seen in this photograph taken at Carstairs mpd on 16 July 1955. The engine had to be set with precision on the turntable, otherwise the effort required would have been too great. Round the edge of the turntable pit is a well-worn wooden track with raised treads to assist the hard-worked railwayman.

From 1949 until 1960 Carstairs was coded 64D, then in the latter year it came under the control of Polmadie and was recoded 66E. In the background one of Carstairs's two 'WD' Class 2-10-0s, No 90753, can be seen. *W. A. C. Smith*

Perth's 'Black Five' No 45474, coaled to capacity, being turned at Ferryhill shed, Aberdeen, in March 1965. The engine shed at Ferryhill was opened in 1908 by the Caledonian Railway, who shared it with the North British; for years this arrangement was a cause of some friction between the two. Their successors continued to share facilities, although the LNER had a shed at Kittybrewster, on the north side of the city. Gradually, however, locomotives of the former LNER began to predominate, even to the point where, on 29 May 1955, 'V2' Class No 60824 headed the 3.30 pm 'West Coast Postal' from Aberdeen; by December 1956 it was regularly booked to 'V2s'. Ferryhill had a few of its own 'Black Fives', however - at mid-November 1959 it had five (Nos 44703, 44794, 45162, 45167, 45469), and four (all but No 45167) two years later. *D. J. Hucknall*

3. Sheds

The size and shape of the British engine shed was wide indeed, ranging from small, single-road sub-sheds at places such as Helston and Aberfeldy to very large depots such as York, Edge Hill, St Margarets, Newton Heath and Eastfield in their heyday.

The individual type often reflected the history of the shed. The LMS in England acquired some 19th-century roundhouses from the Midland Railway (until the late 1940s Leicester had the original Midland Counties Railway engine roundhouse dating from the mid-1850s). In Scotland the company also inherited sheds from the Caledonian, Highland and Glasgow & South Western concerns.

The LNER's legacy probably dated from the 1860s (St Margarets depot had its origins in the site used by the embryo North British Railway in 1846 to store some engines prior to the opening of the line).

The GWR fared much better. As an early pioneer of standardised designs, it built Churchward straight sheds at Banbury (1908), Penzance (1914) and Aberbeeg (1919), for example, and Churchward turntable sheds at locations such as Old Oak Common (1906, four turntables) and St Philips Marsh (1910, double turntable).

Time, corrosive gases from the engines and general wear and tear wrought havoc with the old sheds, particularly those of the 'north-light' pattern. (The Scottish sheds, usually built to higher standards, seemed to survive better.) Late-19th-century sheds were ridiculously inadequate for 20th-century engines and practice. The LMS and LNER, in particular, began drastic remedial action. The latter company got off to a flying start and, by the 1930s, had improved its facilities enormously.

The LMS was more studied in its approach, and analysed the situation carefully before launching into the modernisation programme. After a tentative start (Royston and Nuneaton), the LMS became officially committed to modernisation of many of its sheds in May 1933. Over a period of six years more than 40 sheds were reroofed, and coaling and ash plants were installed.

E. S. Beavor (in *Steam Motive Power Depots*, Ian Allan 1983) reports a thwarted modernisation attempt at Trafford Park. Apparently the gas-lit shed was converted to electric lighting by the LMS. Work was only just completed when a Gas Board official appeared with an old contract obliging the railway to take gas for many years. As a result the new fittings were stripped and gas mains replaced.

From an operational point of view roundhouse sheds were better than the straight-through type. They were safer, and a locomotive could be placed on any vacant road. They allowed work on an engine to be carried out in relative comfort, affording more protection from the winter winds that would whistle through straight sheds. Unfortunately, in some cases, as locomotive and turntable size increased, they became cramped and inadequate.

There can be no doubt, however, that in the end British Railways concluded that the roundhouse was the most efficient type of railway shed. But time was running out, and the promise of 1950s projects such as the Crewe North roundhouse was never fulfilled. They were 'altered, curtailed, rethought and cut back' (Hawkins et al, *BR Engine Sheds, London Midland Matters*).

The last shed to be built was at Thornaby. It was opened in June 1958 and could deal with 220 large locomotives. It was planned as a steam shed with two roundhouses, but in light of the Modernisation Plan it was decided that the cost could not be justified, and one roundhouse was replaced with a straight shed.

The flimsy structures that now serve as service and maintenance areas for diesel locomotives can never have the character, the atmosphere or the tradition of the steam locomotive shed. A large railway shed was a focal point for a whole community.

A little light drizzle falls on an appealing Class 'J10' 0-6-0 No 65204 (an ex-Manchester, Sheffield & Lincolnshire Railway locomotive) as she stands quietly outside the shed at Trafford Park. Smoke from the chimney wafts down on to the sagging, debris-strewn tracks. The dilapidated roof, gas-lamps and general air of inactivity and neglect are not a promising start for the railways of post-war Britain. *R. G. Duckworth*

By 1965 it was a mere shadow of what it had been, but Perth shed always delighted me and I would take any opportunity to visit it. In 1950 138 locomotives were allocated there, the number falling to 97 in 1959. Perth in its heyday was described by G. H. Robin (*Trains Illustrated*, February 1957): 'With so much changing of engines there are plenty of movements to and from the sheds. Stanier 5s from St Rollox, Inverness, Aberdeen and Dundee deal with most workings. . . Aberdeen trains are usually the province of ex-LMS or (BR) Standard types but, at times, Ferryhill shed turns out a "V2" - even an A2 Pacific on occasions. Most interesting "strangers" are the Pacifics working in from Haymarket and Crewe.'

Here a typical variety of locomotives can be seen, including rebuilt 'Patriot' No 45512 *Bunsen*, 'A4' Class No 60006 *Sir Ralph Wedgwood*, a 'B1' and several 'Black Fives'. The line in the foreground led to the repair shop, whilst the brick building behind housed the shed's offices. Locomotive springs are leaning against the barrier, while the area in front of No 45423 is covered with brake shoes. *D. J. Hucknall*

Above One of the 'A2' 'Pacifics', designed by A. H. Peppercorn, No 60530 *Sayajirao*, moves past Dundee Tay Bridge mpd (62B) on its way from the coaling stage to the turntable. Only four of Peppercorn's 'A2s' (Nos 60526/33/38/39) were stationed outside Scotland. The rest were allo-cated to the depots (61B, 62B and 64B) that served the Edinburgh-Aberdeen line.

In early 1958 more than 70 steam locomotives were allocated to Tay Bridge, including two 'A2s' (Nos 60527 *Sun Chariot* and 60528 *Tudor Minstrel*) and several 'V2s'. They were used on the through Aberdeen-Edinburgh trains, includ-ing the night 'Aberdonian'. From September of that year, however, engine-changing on these services was abolished and every express was worked throughout by either a 61B 'A2' or 'V2' or a Haymarket 4-6-2 of any type. *D. J. Hucknall*

Left Dundee Tay Bridge shed was built by the North British Railway. Although re-roofed using the ubiquitous corrugated sheet and its original smoke vents replaced by the open type shown here, very little changed in the structure and lay-out from the 1930s to the 1960s. Changes there were, of course, most notably in the locomotive allocation (101 in 1950, 29 in 1965) and type. Here, in May 1966, are two examples spanning the years, 'J37' No 64608 and Class 'A2' No 60530 *Sayajirao* once more. Tay Bridge shed had 11 'J37s' at the Grouping in 1923 (it still had 10 examples 'on shed' on 16 April 1964, accord-ing to a contemporary issue of *The Railway Observer*) but its passenger locomotive allocation changed considerably with an influx of 'V2s', 'B1s' and some 'A2s'. Indeed, No 60530 was the first engine I saw at 62B on 6 March 1965, on my first visit to the shed. Polished and elegant, she was being coaled; the time was 12.50 pm. *W. A. C. Smith*

Above Fraserburgh station lay 46⅞ miles from Maud Junction in the very north-east corner of Scotland. In this photograph BR Standard Class '2' 2-6-0 No 78045 (a Kittybrewster engine) is seen at Fraserburgh shed on 21 August 1958; it would later work a freight to Maud.

Three years before this photograph was taken, W. A. A. Bremner (*Trains Illustrated*, October 1955) published an article describing traffic and loco-motive working on the Buchan line. He reported that three engines were then usually shedded overnight at Fraserburgh to work passenger trains and freights, and 'almost every possible combination of BR Standard 2-6-4 tanks, B1s, B12s and K2s have appeared on Buchan fish trains'. *W. A. C. Smith*

Below Crieff had once been significant on the railway map. Until 1951 it lay at the junction of the line from Perth to Lochearnhead and the branch from Gleneagles to Crieff. In November of that year, however, passenger traffic between Perth and Crieff and between Comrie and Balquhidder Junction was withdrawn. In this photo-graph, taken on 16 July 1956, Pickersgill '3P' 4-4-0 No 54500 stands outside one of the two engine sheds at Crieff, which had been built by the two railway companies associated with the town in the mid-19th century. Neither shed was big enough to accommodate a typical largish engine and tender.

R. D. Stephen, writing of Crieff in LMS days (*Trains Illustrated*, April 1956), said of the shed in the picture: 'In order to align the chimney with the smoke outlet, the tender had to protrude from the back of the shed; and the track was such that it tilted up a steep hill with the buffers buried in a grass bank.' *W. A. C. Smith*

Above Work is in progress at Boat of Garten shed on 'K2' Class 2-6-0 No 61793 and McIntosh '3F' No 57634 as the 9.45 am Inverness to Glasgow/Edinburgh approaches headed by No 45472 on 31 August 1955. Boat of Garten was on a branch radiating from Keith and, from the North, it was approached by what at first appeared to be a double track but was in fact two parallel single tracks. Freight traffic was worked mostly by 'K2s' and 'D40' 4-4-0s. In the '50s Boat of Garten had two freights per day. One, leaving Keith Junction at 12.40 pm, went up to Aviemore, then the locomotive returned to spend the night at Boat of Garten shed in company with a 'D40' which worked the passenger service of three trains to Craigellachie and back. *W. A. C. Smith*

Below Hamilton was a coal-mining district opposite Motherwell on the south bank of the River Clyde, and the Caledonian Railway built a locomotive depot there on a site to the north of Hamilton West station.

In this evening scene on 18 June 1959 the lowering sun illuminates two former Caledonian engines 'on shed' at Hamilton. By any standards the Drummond '2F' 0-6-0 No 57335 is dirty, its front number-plate unreadable. Even the scorch marks on the smokebox door are gradually disappearing under the grime. In marginally better condition, one of the shed's McIntosh '3P' 0-6-0 tank engines, No 56360, faces into the shed, its work for the day completed. *W. A. C. Smith*

Above The railway shed at Seafield occupied a site between the sea and the Portobello to Leith road. In 1964/65 I would walk past the site regularly, but by then the sidings were invariably deserted although a working water column with a stove heater still stood.

The origins of the shed lay in an incredibly speculative venture whereby the Caledonian Railway had attempted to attract traffic generated by Leith Docks away from the North British Railway. It opened in 1902, but ten years later the CR let the building to the NBR, and it lay derelict until the Second World War when the LNER outstationed freight locomotives there to relieve congestion at 64A.

'Leith Docks shed' was closed in October 1962, but this photograph, taken looking north on 25 August of that year, shows an ex-NBR 'J37'

Class No 64599. Also on shed at the time were 'J37s' Nos 64603/5, 'J36' No 65327 and 'J38s' Nos 65922/29. Dumped were 'V2' No 60825, 'V3' Nos 67605/6/49 and 'N15' Nos 69135/50. *W. A. C. Smith*

Below The light in the month of April is wonderful for railway photography. Here, on 15 April 1963, Holbeck's 'Jubilee' No 45659 *Drake* is shown storming past Dumfries shed, heading towards Annan and Carlisle with an up relief to the 'Thames-Clyde Express'. In the shed yard stands 'Black Five' No 45373 (then a Springs Branch, Wigan, locomotive), another unidentifiable 'Black Five' and a BR Standard 2-6-0. Such is the quality of the light that even the two men over by the shed stand out clearly. *W. A. C. Smith*

Left Standing outside the sub-shed at Alloa on 5 June 1954 is Class 'J88' shunter No 68346. In the mid-1930s Alloa's two 'J88s' were the responsibility of Stirling shed, but when it became a sub-shed of Dunfermline, Alloa's allocation was also officially transferred.

As the NBR's Class 'F', the 'J88s' were, from their introduction through to the Grouping, that railway's standard light shunter. Their appearance was delightful: their small boilers (maximum outside diameter 3 ft 10 in) was surmounted by a very long, slender chimney. They also had dumb buffers that added to the air of eccentricity in the tradition of the small British tank engine.

The first 'J88' to be scrapped was No 68341, which ran out of control and toppled into Kirkcaldy harbour in November 1954 while dealing with a grossly overweight train on the 1 in 25 branch. No 68346 itself was built at Cowlairs in July 1912. It lasted until October 1962 when it was withdrawn to make way for diesel shunters. *K. C. H. Fairey*

Below In a scene that would have remained unchanged from the beginning of the century, an attractive group of old engines stands at St Boswells on the evening of 12 June 1954. At the platform Worsdell Class 'G5' 0-4-4T No 67268, of Tweedmouth shed, waits to work the 7.15 pm train to Berwick along the Tweedside line, which ran through the belt of rich farmland between the Tweed and the Cheviot Hills and served Roxburgh, Kelso, Cornhill-on-Tweed and Norham. The 'G5s' were built by the North Eastern Railway in the period 1894-1901.

In the yard of the stone-built shed (a sub-shed of Hawick) stand two ex-North British Railway engines, 'J36' Class (built between 1888 and 1901) No 65331 obscuring a Class 'J35' (designed by Reid and introduced 1906-19). *W. A. C. Smith*

Coal up, empties back: by far the most important mineral carried on the Midland route south of Leeds was coal. It was hauled along the Erewash valley to Toton sidings where it was sorted and then re-dispatched to the South. The coal came from the pits along or near the line; within a few miles of the Midland line at Rotherham there were several including Rotherham Main, Treeton Main, Aldwarke, Kilnhurst and New Stubbin collieries. From sorting sidings at Roundwood and Masborough, for example, the trains were pulled by engines from Toton, Westhouses, Canklow, Hasland and Royston sheds.

This coal and other freight originating in the Sheffield area required 9,000 wagons daily. Before the introduction of '9Fs' in the mid-1950s, Fowler '4F' 0-6-0s and Stanier '8F' 2-8-0s provided by various sheds were the mainstay of the mineral traffic; later they were supplemented by 'Austerity' 2-8-0s.

Three types of heavy freight locomotives are seen here standing outside Canklow shed on 12 April 1964. An unidentified '9F' is buffered up to '8F' No 48368 (fitted with a Fowler 3,500-gallon tender), and 'Austerity' 2-8-0 No 90122 completes the line. In the right background work is being carried out in the colliery siding on a small saddle tank.

Canklow shed opened in 1900. It was an austere brick-built structure with two parallel pitched roofs, and locomotive accommodation was in the form of a roundhouse with a 55-foot turntable. The Midland Railway laid great stress on standardisation and, in this photograph, showing the southerly end of the shed, unmistakeably Midland features can be seen. On the left-hand side of the picture is the sandhouse; its chimney was a design that could be seen from Hellifield to Gloucester. In the background is a typical Midland water tank on its brick support.

For as long as I could remember Canklow had never cleaned its locomotives particularly well - as long as the number could be read was all that seemed necessary - but by the 1960s there were just too few staff anyway. By late December 1964 Canklow's establishment consisted of 124 drivers, 40 passed firemen, 56 firemen, 12 passed cleaners and 27 maintenance staff. *D. J. Hucknall*

Above The immediate post-war years must have been grim on Britain's railways. They inherited a legacy of labour shortages and badly maintained structures and locomotives. This undated photograph taken at Lostock Hall shows the utter dereliction of the roof. The LMS had planned to re-roof the structure in 1947 (by which time it would have been in place for 65 years), but it was eventually dealt with in 1953. Incredibly, looking at this photograph, Lostock Hall lasted as a steam shed until August 1968.

Standing amidst the debris is '4F' No 44151 (a Holbeck engine in 1947 but eventually moved to Nottingham) with the hybrid livery (BR number, LMS tender) of the period and fitted with a Deeley parallel chimney. *R. G. Duckworth*

Left Blackpool had two sheds which had originated in the days of the Lancashire & Yorkshire Railway. In this photograph, 'Black Five' No 45102 (24E) is seen at Blackpool (Central) mpd. I had always associated the code 24E with Blackpool and, indeed, apart from a short period (1950-April 1952) when it became 28A, it maintained that shed number until September 1963 when it became 10B. In 1950 Blackpool's allocation had been over 60 locomotives, falling to about 40 in 1959. It included several 'Jubilees', two of which (Nos 45571 *South Africa* and 45574 *India*) arrived in 1937 and remained Blackpool engines until late 1963. Central shed was eventually closed in November 1964, although its allocation had been removed in the previous September. *D. J. Hucknall*

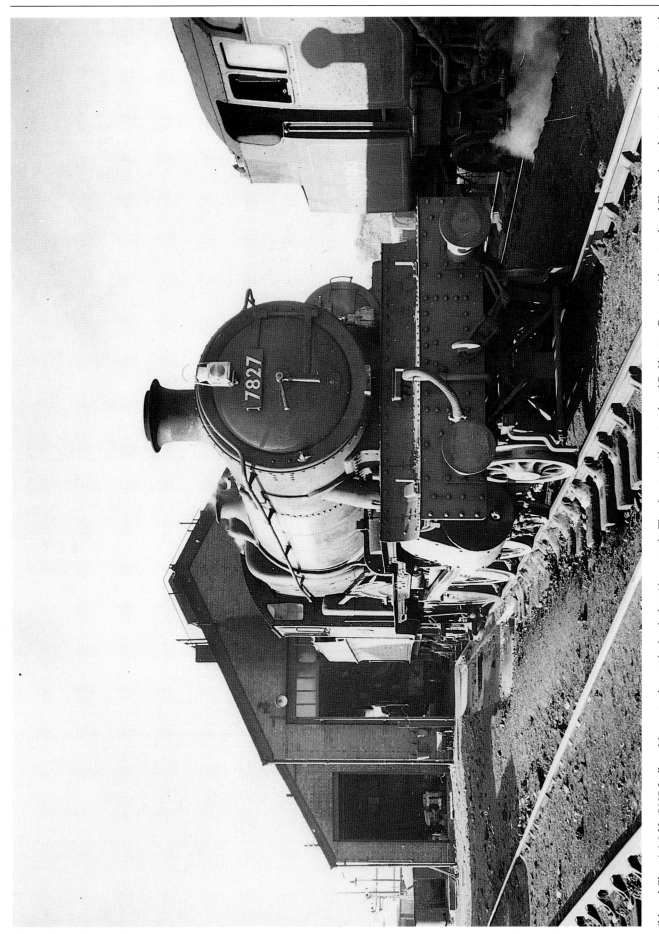

'Manor' Class 4-6-0 No 7827 *Lydham Manor* stands outside the shed at Aberystwyth. This depot was a brick-build, two-road sub-shed of Machynlleth. The 'Cambrian Coast Express' (reintroduced in 1954 after a gap of 28 years) ran between Aberystwyth and Paddington. Between Aberystwyth and Shrewsbury the train used to be entrusted to Machynlleth's best 'Manor'. Even in 1964 the engine involved would be polished and sometimes have white-painted buffers and smokebox-door hinge-straps. *D. J. Hucknall Collection*

Helston, at the end of the branch from Gwinear Road station on the Penzance-Plymouth line, was British Railways' most southerly terminus. It was a sub-shed of Penzance and was used to house the branch-line locomotive overnight. In this photograph '45XX' Class 2-6-2T No 4566 reverses from the shed into Helston station in August 1957. On this day I had caught a bus at what had been the GWR Coverack Road Motor Halt to Helston. I then travelled up the branch to Gwinear Road for a few hours' trainspotting. *D. J. Hucknall*

Below The engine shed and yard at Yeovil were often full of locomotives. Constrained by a stream on the south side, the station to the north and a road to the east, however, they were also cramped and awkward to work in. Yeovil's allocation was relatively small, but included ex-SR 2-6-0s that worked mixed traffic trains to Salisbury, Exeter and Portsmouth, as well as engines that came over on the closure of the former Great Western shed at Pen Mill. It was not unusual either to see 'light Pacifics' in and around the shed.

In this photograph, taken on 16 May 1964, 'U' Class No 31632, an unidentified ex-GWR tank engine and a 'light Pacific' stand in the yard. Until the late 1940s locos were coaled by men wielding huge shovels. When the crane shown on the left arrived shed life became a little easier, coaling being carried out using half-ton tubs. The crane could also dash around clearing clinker and ash. *K. C. H. Fairey*

Sun streams into the motive power depot at Cambridge on 23 April 1962 illuminating one of the sturdy Worsdell 'J15' Class locomotives, No 65469. Built in May 1912 for the Great Eastern Railway, she lasted until August 1962. In true Great Eastern style, she has a stovepipe chimney; the work was carried out at her home shed of Norwich by cutting the top off the standard LNER chimney. In April 1961 No 65469 had the distinction of being the last steam engine to run on the Wickham Market-Framlingham branch line. *K. C. H. Fairey*

Left Moving from the yard into the shed, here we see an ex-NBR Holmes 'J36' (possibly No 65282), a type introduced in 1888, standing in the deep, dark recesses at St Margarets. The gloom and dilapidation was so typical of structures which had remained virtually unaltered since the beginning of the century. It remains an abiding tribute to the dedication of the shed staff that any serviceable locomotive ever appeared from some of our engine depots. *D. J. Hucknall*

Below Today's preserved steam sheds generally present a less gloomy image. Didcot shed was a standard four-road depot opened in June 1932, built under the provisions of the Loans and Guarantees Act (1929). It is now used by the Great Western Society to rebuild, repair and house some of its wonderful collection of locomotives. This photograph, taken on the afternoon of Saturday 20 April 1991, could almost have been taken shortly after its opening in the 1930s. 'Castle' Class No 5029 *Nunney Castle* and 'King' Class No 6024 *King Edward I* stand, out of steam, undergoing adjustments. *D. J. Hucknall*

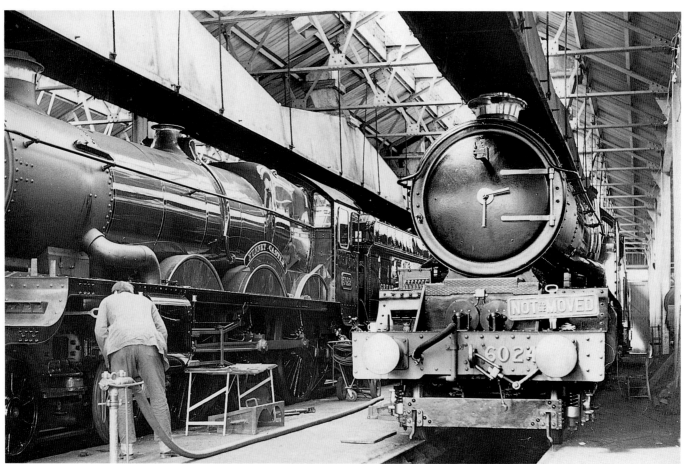

Above A delightful view of the inside of Tweedmouth shed on 12 June 1954 showing Worsdell 'J25' Class No 65727 and Gresley 'J39s' Nos 64941 and 64868. At Tweedmouth the NER branch to Coldstream and thence to Kelso, Roxburgh and St Boswells started. There was also a line to Wooler and eventually to Alnwick and Alnmouth. The 'J39s' were used extensively on the branches together with a couple of 'J72' tanks. In 1955 British Railways began to destroy the Tweedside branch by halving the number of trains and closing stations.

Nevertheless, Tweedmouth shed flourished. At the beginning of December 1959 its allocation included one Ivatt 2-6-0 (No 46476), four 'B1s' (Nos 61025, 61199, 61241, 61322), eight 'K3s' (Nos 61854, 61901/17/30/34/52/69/85) and 13 'J39s' (Nos 64711, 64813/43/44/68/97, 64916/17/24/25/29/41/49).

Compared to straight sheds such as those just encountered, roundhouses always seemed light and airy. Certainly they appeared to resist better the ravages of years of corrosive gases. *W. A. C. Smith*

Below From Saturday 1 February 1958 the Midland Region main line from Chesterfield to Darfield came under the control of the Eastern Region. Depots at Grimesthorpe (19A), Millhouses (19B) and Canklow (19C) were also transferred and became 41B, 41C and 41D respectively. Dr Les Nixon, who must have been one of my contemporaries in our trainspotting days in South Yorkshire, pointed out (*Classic Steam: Les Nixon*, SLP) that when this change took place we trainspotters were quite put out. Certainly my Canklow was 19C not 41D, and had '2Fs', '3Fs' and '8Fs', not 'B1s' and 'Austerities'.

Inside the roundhouse at Canklow shed on 22 May 1965, '8F' Class 2-8-0 No 48279 stands with safety valves blowing and the injector opened. *D. J. Hucknall*

Above The roundhouse at Canklow in its Eastern Region days, with '8F' No 48214 and one of Canklow's 'B1s', No 61050, facing the turntable. The light, streaming through the roof and windows, transforms this mundane scene. *D. J. Hucknall*

Left Because of the huge growth in coal traffic that resulted from the building of the coal staiths at Blyth, it was necessary to have a shed on both sides of the river. The depot at South Blyth was completed in 1879, while North Blyth was opened in 1897 to eliminate excessive locomotive movement, and consisted of a rectangular building containing a central turntable and 22 radiating roads. In this photograph of the interior of North Blyth shed, every engine in sight is a 'J27', that immediately to the right of the entrance being No 65801.

The two sheds, together with that at Percy Main, handled the bulk of the coal traffic in the Blyth area. A typical stint of duty for 'J27' No 65893 in the 1950s from a guard's journal (see J. A. Wells, *The Blyth and Tyne Branch 1874-1989*, Northumberland County Library 1990) would be leaving the shed at 6.15 am, then trips to the collieries at Lynemouth, Bedlington, Choppington and Lynemouth again, with empties. In between, runs from the pits to the staiths were made with loaded wagons. At the end of the crew's shift the 'J27' returned to the shed at 2.40 pm for coal, water and fire cleaning before the next shift took over. *D. J. Hucknall*

Neglected and filthy in the gloom of North Blyth, three Ivatt Class '4' 2-6-0 locomotives stand 'dead' on the turntable in July 1967. During its working life, No 43123 had been allocated to Hull Dairycoates and West Hartlepool. No 43050 was shedded at Bradford (Manningham) from April 1960 to April 1967 and may well have been in store at this time, awaiting its final journey to the scrapyard at Hughes Bolckows Ltd in Blyth. D. J. Hucknall

Above left The '61s' were predominantly suburban passenger engines that worked in the London area from sheds such as Old Oak Common, Slough, Oxford and Reading, and without a doubt they were handsome engines in their lined green livery. They were the staple engines on local services - Reading to Newbury, Paddington to Henley, Oxford to Didcot - bustling along and emitting a whistling noise as they free-wheeled.

Here No 6120 stands burnished inside one of Old Oak Common's (81A) roundhouses. She was allocated to Old Oak Common when new in late 1931, and remained there for almost the whole of her working career. In October 1960 she was moved to Didcot and was withdrawn from there in April 1962. *D. J. Hucknall collection*

Left Large engine sheds could be cold, dark and slightly menacing. On other occasions they could be transformed by shafts of sunlight into places of enchantment. Here four 'Castle' Class locomotives face one of the turntables in Old Oak Common shed, the silence broken only by a hiss of escaping steam from No 5034 *Corfe Castle* as she comes to rest. No 5087 *Tintern Abbey* and No 5077 *Fairey Battle* stand cold and out of steam. *H. G. Usmar*

Above Tank engines, and particularly pannier tanks, were used extensively by the Great Western throughout its area. In 1948 British Railways acquired 2,436 tank engines from the GWR, of which 1,251 were 0-6-0Ts. Here, in a quiet moment inside one of the roundhouses at Old Oak Common, three tank engines are disposed round the turntable. '57XX' Class No 8768 (an example of an amazingly numerous class, introduced in 1933 and built until 1947), '94XX' Class 2-6-2T (introduced in 1947) No 9423, and '61XX' Class 2-6-2T (introduced in 1931 for passenger workings in the London suburban area) No 6135 typify excellently GWR small locomotive design as they stand side by side. Examples of both the '61XX' and '57XX' Classes are preserved, but the last '94XX' I saw was No 9405 when I was at Paddington station on 23 February 1965. *H. G. Usmar*

4. Shed yards

The yard of a major steam depot was an unforgettable sight. Close to, one was overwhelmed by the sheer size and power of the locomotive. The bustle of weekday working or the relative calm of a Sunday morning were best appreciated at a distance.

From a well-chosen vantage point, track after track, branching and branching again, leading into the shed buildings, might be seen. There would be rows of engines, some cold, some quietly simmering under a haze of smoke. Here and there, men would be working - standing on the tender trimming the coal, shovelling ash and clinker, operating a turntable - or talking. Occasionally the metallic clanking and the rushing roar and thump from a mechanical coaler fuelling a locomo- tive would be heard.

Many years after their disappearance, it is easy to recall the sheds - Sundays at Penzance, with row upon row of 'Halls' and 'Granges' standing quietly in the summer sun after working specials into the town; Kingmoor yard in the mid-1960s, quiet when compared to a few years earlier, yet stacked with 'Britannias' and 'Black Fives', with here and there an 'A3', an 'A4', 'Patriots', 'Standards' - the variety seemed endless.

Today I try to recapture the atmosphere of a working shed at places such as Didcot or Ropley, where the shed yard still remains the focus of purposeful activity. Although the activity is on a smaller scale, the dedica- tion of the men remains as great.

A typical scene at Perth shed (63A), with one of its ubiquitous, worked- stained 'Black Fives', is transformed by a flash of sunlight after a sudden spring shower. Against the stark blackness of the shed interior the drifting steam serves as a reminder of the wonderful atmosphere of the steam loco- motive shed and yard. *D. J. Hucknall*

'Britannia' Class 4-6-2 No 70007 *Coeur de Lion* was one of several that were introduced to the Great Eastern section of British Railways in 1951/2. They were highly regarded in East Anglia and, until displaced by diesels, they worked trains between London and Norwich, often covering 500 miles daily on double return trips. Attitudes were different, however, elsewhere, and from Polmadie to Newton Abbot they were accepted unenthusiastically.

In this photograph No 70007 stands, minus its nameplates, in the yard at 63A in the spring of 1965 with 'Black Five' No 45475. The right-hand-side injector of the 'Britannia' is working vigorously and its safety valves are blowing. Dangling through an open window of the cab, the locomotive's 'pet pipe' - used for cleaning the footplate and damping dusty coal - dribbles water on to the ground below. *D. J. Hucknall*

Left Gateshead's 'A4s' Nos 60005 *Sir Charles Newton*, 60016 *Silver King*, 60019 *Bittern* and 60023 *Golden Eagle* were officially transferred to the Scottish Region on 5 November 1963. Initially, however, Nos 60016/19 continued to work from Gateshead. *Bittern*, for example, pulled the up 'Northumbrian' on 15 November and was frequently seen at the head of freight trains. She was being repaired at Heaton on almost the last day of that month.

On arrival in Scotland No 60019 was stored at Kittybrewster, but towards the middle of 1964 she was reactivated and worked on the Glasgow-Aberdeen trains with her sisters. When this photograph was taken at Perth in mid-August 1964, *Bittern* looked as if her working days were almost over. She was not withdrawn, however, until the end of the summer of 1966 and then not before she had headed a special on 3 September to mark the last public run of an 'A4' on Scottish Region metals. *D. J. Hucknall*

Below Two locomotives with very different histories stand side-by-side in Perth shed yard on an April evening in 1965. Riddles Class '4' 2-6-4T No 80092 was built at Brighton Works and entered service on 9 October 1954 at Kentish Town. Gresley 'A4' No 60024 *Kingfisher* emerged from the Works at Doncaster and began work at King's Cross on 8 July 1937. No 80092, after hurrying commuters and stock in and out of St Pancras, eventually worked the branch from Killin to Killin Junction in the beautiful surroundings of Loch Tay, while after years of East Coast Main Line express work based at Haymarket (9 May 1939-9 September 1963), No

60024's last stints involved demanding work on the Aberdeen-Glasgow line.

A plaque can be seen on the side of *Kingfisher*. I could never understand at the time why a green diamond should be attached to a locomotive, but I now know that it had once depicted a kingfisher and had been designed and made by Lieutenant A. F. Mortimer RN of Donibristle. It was unveiled at a ceremony at Haymarket on 21 October 1954. I wonder if the official who authorised the obliteration realised that yet another link between the railways and the community had been cut. *D. J. Hucknall*

Above Eastfield shed, Glasgow, was opened by the North British Railway in September 1904. Almost 60 years later, on 12 September 1962, 'B1s' Nos 61396 (65A until January 1963) and 61398 (64A) stand in the yard at the north end of the shed with Class 'J37' No 64623 (65A). The latter's tender is being filled from the water column and already the excess water is cascading on to the track. Behind the locomotives is the 500-ton capacity coaling plant build in the 1930s. To the left of No 61396 is what appears to be the remains of Eastfield's original manual coaling stage. *W. A. C. Smith*

Below Every engine in sight is an ex-Caledonian Railway locomotive in this view of the yard at the north end of Motherwell shed on 14 May

1955. In the foreground are Pickersgill '3P' Class 4-4-0s Nos 54464/65, behind the former is McIntosh '3F' No 57593 and, behind that, is a Pickersgill '3F' No 57681. Of the two types of '3F', the McIntosh design was the more efficient; the locomotives did a fair amount of passenger work and could be seen frequently on both Edinburgh and Glasgow suburban services. They were also a very common sight on freight trains around Motherwell. No 57681 survived until January 1964 when it was sold for scrap to T. W. Ward at Inverkeithing. It had seen service in many parts of Scotland, having been allocated at various times to Ayr, Hurlford, Ardrossan, Stirling, Carstairs, Wick and, of course, Motherwell. *W. A. C. Smith*

Above Smoke from McIntosh '3F' No 57572 covers 'Crab' 2-6-0 No 42879 and 'Black Five' No 45007 at Hurlford (67B) on Saturday 18 April 1964. Approximately 2 miles south of Kilmarnock station, the shed had been erected by the Glasgow & South Western Railway at a point where the main line to Carlisle diverged from the line to Darvel, Dumfries and Annan. In the 1950s and early '60s 67B had over 50 engines; in late October 1961, for example, it boasted 11 '2P' 4-4-0s, six 'Crabs' (Nos 42735/39/43/44/46 and 42880), three '4Fs', seven 'Black Fives' (Nos 45007/10/45124/92/45266/45467/89), seven Drummond '2Fs' and 11 McIntosh '3Fs'. It also had Standard Class '3s' (77015-19).

Although Corkerhill (67A) was the principal mpd for Glasgow (St Enoch) station, Hurlford provided the pilot for the up 'Thames-Clyde Express' as far as Kilmarnock or New Cumnock. The 9.25 am St Enoch-Dumfries was also a 67B turn. Other Hurlford workings involved freight and passenger trains between Kilmarnock and Dumfries, and Kilmarnock and Ayr and Girvan. *W. A. C. Smith*

Left A fine array of locomotives stands in the shed yard at Dumfries on 29 October 1955. Visible in this view from the Annan Road overbridge are Fowler '2P' 4-4-0 No 40577 and a sister engine, a '4F' and two 'Crabs'. The 'Crabs', once the mainstay of the Dumfries-Stranraer freight trains, were removed from the depot by July 1964 to be replaced by the ubiquitous 'Black Fives'.

As built by the Glasgow & South Western Railway, Dumfries shed once had a splendid row of many-paned windows where the bricked part of the upper elevation is seen; they were removed in 1947. *W. A. C. Smith*

Above The pagoda-like tops to the smoke outlets on some of the ex-North British Railway sheds were an inspired embellishment. I saw them first here at Thornton Junction shed (62A) and was completely charmed. Here we see 'D30' 4-4-0 No 62442 *Simon Glover* and 'J37' No 64581 on 18 August 1954. Thornton provided engines for, among other duties, freight workings connected with the Fifeshire coalfield. This shot is absolutely packed with fascinating details - the scorched smokebox of the 'J37', the ashpit guard rails and the complete litter of shovels and fire irons to the side of *Simon Glover* - all rather disreputably bent.

Oddly, many steam depots had sidings with slightly obscure names.

62A had an absolutely fascinating example - it was called 'The Fat Wife'. *W. A. C. Smith*

Below The roof at Polmont locomotive shed was similarly adorned with the pagoda-topped smoke outlets, and in this photograph taken on 10 September 1955 they add some distinction to a view of another Reid 'J37' Class locomotive, No 64593 (Jan 1919-Nov 1963). Polmont always had a few 'J37s' (Nos 64537/51/70/71, 64636 at mid-December 1959; Nos 64537/70/71 and 64636 in mid-October 1960). Invariably dirty, 'J37s' always gave the impression of being big engines. *W. A. C. Smith*

Above A pair of 'V2s' grace the yard at St Margarets, also in the spring of 1965. On the right-hand side, spectre-like, an English Electric Type 4 diesel stands - a harbinger of changes so soon to come. Even by the summer of 1964 the Type 4s were being used increasingly on the Waverley route, and freights to Carlisle from Niddrie and Millerhill, and local work from Portobello to Hawick, all were rapidly succumbing. *D. J. Hucknall*

Below left Taken at the side of the sand furnace (the wall on the left) at St Margarets, this photograph shows work being carried out on a 'V2' at the end of a run. Clearly shown are the outside steam pipes and the very long cylinder drain cock pipes.

64A received its first 'V2s' early in 1939 with Nos 4815 (60844) and 4819 (60848). At the start of 1965, when this photograph was taken, St

Margarets had eight of the Class. They found regular work on Edinburgh-Perth passenger trains and on goods trains over the Waverley route to Carlisle. *D. J. Hucknall*

Below right Diesels at St Margarets in the summer of 1965. Unlike many devoted followers of steam, I never really minded diesel locomotives - they were a significant part of the contemporary railway scene and therefore deserved to be recorded. Possibly not so much in Scotland, but certainly south of the Border, they were much more photogenic than the rather sad-looking, badly maintained steam specimens they replaced. Many enginemen regarded them as a positive boon - clean, comfortable and responsive. Here an engineman in a steam age uniform strides between two powerful, mixed-traffic diesels - the Brush and English Electric Type 4s. *D. J. Hucknall*

Above In the period of transition between steam and diesel traction on Britain's railways, there never appeared to be any segregation between the two, although their servicing demands were quite different. In continental Europe, because of the susceptibility of diesel locomotives to the abrasive ash and char generated by steam engines, sheds were usually partitioned. At St Margarets, however, on Saturday 13 March 1965, two 'B1s' and an English Electric Type 4 diesel stand side by side.

'B1' No 61076 was borrowed from 64A by Corkerhill shed in the first week of August 1959 and even appeared at Ardrossan (Montgomery Pier) on an Irish boat train. It was withdrawn in September 1965 and broken up at Faslane in the following November. *D. J. Hucknall*

Right In Scotland severe weather can strike locally with unexpected suddenness and it is best to be prepared. For example, on 12 January 1955 the worst blizzard for 25 years struck Caithness and Sutherland. During the night of 16/17 February snowstorms returned, stranding several trains in deep snow at places such as Slochd and Tomatin. Even when spring might be expected further south, snow and ice can appear and, on 21 March 1955 the West Coast Main Line between Lockerbie and Ecclefechan was blocked and seven northbound night expresses had to be diverted via the Waverley route.

Possibly remembering earlier episodes and the terrible winter of 1963, sheds that served lines that could be affected fitted small snowploughs to several of their locomotives. Here, at St Margarets in February 1965, Kingmoor's 'Black Five' No 45138 and St Margarets's own 'J39' No 65929, both Waverley route regulars, occupy adjacent tracks between duties. *D. J. Hucknall*

We sometimes forget how short-lived were some of our steam locomotives. 'B1' Class No 61397, receiving attention at St Margarets on 17 April 1965, had been built by the North British Locomotive Co and only entered service in February 1952. It incorporated many features to aid the enginemen, including a self-cleaning smokebox, a rocker grate and hopper ashpan (the flaps at the bottom of which could be opened to disgorge its contents into the ash pit), a Stone's generator and electric lamps (No 61397 has, however, lost the lamps on her central and right-hand brackets). She was withdrawn in June 1965 and was broken up in Faslane three months later. *D. J. Hucknall*

Above A pair of 'B1s', No 61308 coupled to No 61191, at St Margarets. A full discharge of steam escaping from the safety valves of a locomotive would make the air vibrate and almost crackle, echoing around its confines of the shed yard.

I had left Edinburgh by the time St Margarets was closed in April 1967. I know that, had I returned, the silence of the shed after all the locomotives had gone would have brought a lump to my throat. *D. J. Hucknall*

Right On a Sunday afternoon in the winter of 1965, Standard Class '4' 2-6-4T No 80055 is seen in the yard at Dalry Road shed, Edinburgh. The light was dreadful, the conditions miserable. However, the snow on the ground, reflecting the feeble light, contrasts the locomotive starkly with her surroundings.

No 80055 was built at Derby around late December 1954 or early January 1955. She was allocated to the Scottish Region and, together with Fairburn and other Standard tanks from Hamilton, Motherwell, Carstairs and Greenock, energetically bustled the rush hour trains out of Glasgow Central to the suburbs. *D. J. Hucknall*

Spring seemed to come slowly in 1965 and Sunday 21 March was another drizzly day that year. At Carlisle Kingmoor shed, 'Britannia' Class 4-6-2 No 70040 (formerly *Clive of India*) stands buffered up to an unidentified Class '9F' 2-10-0. No 70040 was out of steam and its smokebox door was open; the '9F', however, was ready for further work. According to my notes at the time, there were at least nine '9Fs' on shed (Nos 92015/23/27/48/56/99/92124/30 and 92233). '9Fs' were first allocated to 12A in the early summer of 1964 when Nos 92009/23/24/54/92115 and 92130 arrived, primarily for use on the Shap to Ravenscraig limestone trains. *D. J Hucknall*

Above A line of 'K1s' at Blyth at 12.57 pm on a summer day in 1966. Peppercorn's 'K1' Class locomotives were built by the North British Locomotive Co, 70 being ordered in 1947. The first batch of 20 was divided equally between Darlington (Nos 62001-10) and Blaydon (Nos 61021-30). A further 20 (Nos 62041-50, 56-65) also went to Darlington. The remainder went to the Eastern Region.

In the 1960s the 'K1s' in the North East took over the colliery duties from withdrawn 'J26s', 'J27s' and 'J39s'. South Blyth mpd was closed to steam on 28 May 1967 whilst the North shed survived until 9 September 1967. *D. J. Hucknall*

Right The thick coating of ash and dust on the driving wheels and coupling rods of 'K1' Class 2-6-0 No 62002 (June 1949 to October 1966) was typical in the depressing period immediately before the elimination of steam on British Railways. The locomotive was photographed with sister engine No 62067 (February 1950 to January 1967) at North Blyth mpd during the summer of 1966. The situation had probably been exacerbated by the fine ash from the hopper ashpan of the 'K1s'; this was operated by a fixed handle that is clearly visible and was often distorted, allowing the ash to dribble out and be blown on to the oil-covered surfaces of the locomotive's motion.

When new, No 62002 was allocated to Darlington, whence it was transferred to Heaton and then to Blaydon. No 62067 was originally shedded at March but moved to the North East in 1962. *D. J. Hucknall*

Other locomotives were in an awful external condition in the final days of steam. Typically, Ivatt 2-6-0 No 43084 stands framed by the entrance to North Blyth shed around 1967. Gone are the number-plate and shedplate (possibly removed by bands of so-called 'enthusiasts' who visited sheds with their spanners and pliers prepared to pilfer), replaced by a crudely chalked number.

Worthy of comment in the left background is Blyth's north coal staith. These timber structures allowed coal to be loaded on to colliers lying alongside on the river. Trains were propelled to the top of the staiths and wagons brought above loading chutes and discharged into the holds. *D. J. Hucknall*

On Saturday 24 June 1967, with only three months remaining before the end of steam locomotive operation in the North East of England, the weeds and sand are beginning to encroach on the depot at North Blyth as two 'J27s' stand coaled and waiting for duty. A characteristic British locomotive designed for heavy mineral haulage, the J27s, according to O. S. Nock (*British Railways in Action*, Nelson 1956) were, to the end, 'hard slogging, honest-to-goodness "colliers" and little else'. *D. J. Hucknall*

LNER 'N5' Class No 69364 (GCR Class '9F') was built for the GCR in July 1900 by Beyer Peacock & Co, one of 129 engines originally built for shunting and goods work over short distances. Over the years they were increasingly used on stopping passenger trains, particularly on the LNER lines in the North West of England between Manchester Central, Warrington, Wigan and Irlam.

In the North West the 'N5s' were shedded at Gorton, Trafford Park, Heaton Mersey, Brunswick, Walton, Northwich, Chester and Wrexham. Unfortunately, the photographer could not remember where or when this shot was taken, but the presence of a 'D11' on the right-hand side would suggest either Heaton Mersey or Trafford Park. As for the date, No 69364 received its British Railways number in January 1949 and was withdrawn in August 1955. *R. G. Duckworth*

Above A boy with a box camera captured this shot of the shed yard at Lostock Hall, Preston. Undated, but probably in the period 1948-51, it shows two former Lancashire & Yorkshire Railway locomotives - an 0-8-0 'Coal Engine', No 52916, and an Aspinall '3F' 0-6-0, No 12588 of 23D (Wigan). Lostock Hall shed opened in 1882 and was adjacent to Lostock Hall station, part of the roof of which can be seen in the left-hand background. The station lay between Bamber Bridge and Midge Hall on the Blackburn-Liverpool line. *R. G. Duckworth*

Left A delightful shot of ex-Lancashire & Yorkshire Railway Aspinall/Barton Wright '2F' 0-6-0ST No 51423 as she stands at Lostock Hall, her home shed. For years the 0-6-0STs were the standard shunting engines of the former L&Y lines, but gradually they were superseded; No 51423 was withdrawn in the period 1958-59. Up to May 1946 Lostock Hall had the code 23E and was a 'garage' of Bank Hall (then 23A). From 1946 it became 24C, under the control of Accrington (24A). *R. G. Duckworth*

Above Edge Hill depot, Liverpool, must have been stunning for enthusiasts. It was massive - 20 roads - and was the main passenger depot for the area. Its allocation was correspondingly large; in 1959 it consisted of 124 locomotives including 13 'Patriots', 11 'Jubilees', 10 'Royal Scots' and seven 'Princess Royals'.

In this fine study, taken outside the 'old' shed on 24 September 1961, the delightful lines of unrebuilt 'Patriot' No 45533 *Lord Rathmore* are shown to very good effect. Blown by a gently westerly wind, drifting smoke forms an evocative backcloth to the engine. *Lord Rathmore* was withdrawn in September 1962, and scrapped one month later at Crewe Works.

Although by 1961 relegated almost to third-rate duties, the Class had previously been used on very demanding work indeed. As I have mentioned elsewhere, I found them immensely appealing. The first of the class I ever saw was No 45538 *Giggleswick*, hurrying through the station at Parkgate & Rawmarsh in a flurry of steam. From that moment I was forever a fan. *K. C. H. Fairey*

Below Another big depot, Newton Heath shed, Manchester (code 26A from 1935 to September 1963), had been the largest shed of the former Lancashire & Yorkshire Railway system. It had 24 roads and throughout most of its existence had a large allocation of steam locomotives (169 in 1945, 119 in November 1961). During the 1930s the LMS carried out an extensive modernisation programme, including the re-roofing of the northern half of the shed.

In this photograph, taken on 9 September 1959, some fascinating details can be seen, including a relic of L&Y days in the form of the curious water column. The metal stem protruding from its top had once supported a gas lamp, but latterly this had been replaced by an electric light. The roof, the 1935/36 replacement of the original L&Y hipped roof, is showing marked signs of dilapidation as a result of almost 25 years' exposure to steam and smoke.

The 'Jubilee' Class locomotive, No 45679 *Armada*, was formerly at Millhouses, but moved to Scotland in the autumn of 1952 as part of a very large north-south reshuffle of these locomotives. By this time, however, it had returned south and was allocated to Crewe North. It retained some remainders of its stay - large cab-side numbers and part of the tablet-catching mechanism. *Armada* was to be stationed at 26A from early June 1960. *A. Swain*

Above A pair of 'V2' Class 2-6-2s, Nos 60828 and 60855, stand at York mpd on 2 May 1964, a day so uniformly grey that the sky was completely featureless.

Designed by Gresley for heavy, fast, long-distance work, the 'V2s' were capable engines indeed, and there are many recorded examples of their substitution for failed locomotives on expresses with the schedule being maintained. On 12 October 1957, for example, the locomotive on the 8 am from Newcastle developed a fault and was replaced by No 60946. The train left Doncaster 15 minutes late yet arrived at King's Cross 8 minutes early.

According to the records, No 60828 was withdrawn in October 1965. They also indicate, however, that No 60855 was withdrawn in April 1964 and was supposedly in store at Darlington when this photograph was taken. *D. J. Hucknall*

Below On that dank May day York Minster was barely visible through the murk drifting across the yard. By 1964 diesel locomotives, particularly the English Electric Type 4s, had begun to predominate and had regular duties to and from York. They were allocated to depots such as Gateshead (52A) and Liverpool (8A). The former shed was responsible for the 9.30 am Glasgow-King's Cross and some Newcastle-Liverpool services as well as the up and down 'Norseman' between London and York. *D. J. Hucknall*

Saltley's Class '4F' 0-6-0 No 44213 stands by the entrance to an apparently deserted Millhouses shed, Sheffield, on 13 August 1960. Millhouses was opened in 1901 and was the largest of the straight sheds built by the Midland Railway, housing passenger locomotives required for the Sheffield area. Coded 19B in 1935, it retained this identification until February 1958 when it became an Eastern Region depot (41C). At the beginning of December 1959 there were 12 'Jubilees' on its allocation, including No 45590 *Travancore* (the first of the Class I can remember seeing) and No 45609 *Gilbert and Ellice Islands* (apart from No 45637, which was irreparably damaged in 1952 in the Harrow disaster, No 45609 was the first of the Class to be withdrawn). Rebuilt 'Patriots' (Nos 45514/36) and 'Royal Scots' (Nos 46131/47/48/51) also came to Millhouses in early 1960. *W. A. C. Smith*

Oswestry shed, opened in 1860, had been the largest depot on the Cambrian Railways. The Cambrian must have been a grim old railway - George Behrend, in his delightful book *Gone with Regret*, points out that its directors had been summoned to the Bar of the House of Commons to receive a reprimand for making their employees work continuously for 23 hours a day.

After the Grouping, the Cambrian became the Central Wales division of the Great Western, retaining Oswestry as its headquarters. The GWR improved the depot, initially in 1929 and again in 1939, when the corrugated sheet roof and large cowls were fitted. In 1948, Oswestry's allocation consisted of 36 locos, including two 'Manors' (Nos 7807/8), five '2251s', four '2300' Class

'Dean Goods' engines, six 'Dukedogs' and sundry other locomotives. By 1959 most of the depot's '2251s' had either gone elsewhere or had been scrapped. No 7808 went to Newton Abbot but 7807 had been joined by Nos 7800/01/09/10/19/22 and 27. The predominant locomotive, however, was the Ivatt 2-6-0 of which there were 15, increasing to 22 by the beginning of the '60s.

In this photograph, taken towards the end of the life of the shed (it was closed in January 1965), two of the ubiquitous Ivatt 2-6-0s are standing in the sunshine outside the depot. Incredibly, even in 1992 the external facade of the former Cambrian Railways Works is relatively unaltered from steam days. *D. J. Hucknall collection*

Above Aberystwyth mpd was set at the end of the station in the fork between the line to Machynlleth and the 58-mile long branch line to Carmarthen. It opened in 1864, but when the station was rebuilt in 1925, the GWR improved the shed. Then in 1938 it was demolished and a brick building erected as a replacement.

From 1932 Aberystwyth had been a sub-shed of Machynlleth. In 1948 it had among its allocation of 16 locomotives five '2251s' and six 'Dukedog'

4-4-0s (small hybrids of the 'Bulldog' and 'Duke' Class locomotives). Some 11 years later, on 4 April 1959, '2251' Class 2-6-0 No 2260 (at Aberystwyth even in 1948) and '4300' Class 2-6-0 No 6371 are seen standing outside the shed. The '2251s' hauled freight trains over the Cambrian for many years until replaced in the 1960s by more powerful engines. The '4300s' similarly rumbled along with passenger trains until displaced by the 'Manors' and Standard Class '4' 4-6-0s. *K. C. H. Fairey*

Right '54XX' Class 0-6-0T No 5424 is seen at Banbury shed (84C) on 6 August 1958. Designed by Charles Collett for push-and-pull working, the '54XXs' were introduced in 1931. No 5424 was a relatively long serving member of 84C, having certainly been there in January 1944. She was used on trips such as the Princes Risborough and High Wycombe auto-trains.

Behind the tank engine is the coal stage supporting a 45,000-gallon water tank. To the left, partially dismantled, is one of the shed's ash-dropping shelters; these were erected during the Second World War to prevent the glow from dropped ash being spotted by enemy aircraft. *D. J. Hucknall*

Above Against a background dominated by the shed's coaler, BR Standard Class '4' 2-6-4T No 80067 (1C, Watford) stands at Willesden depot on 23 April 1959. Willesden, five and a half miles from Euston, provided engines for main-line freight and some passenger trains; it was also a repair depot for Camden, Watford and Bletchley. Noteworthy in the photograph is the large number of tall poles, each carrying two lamps, which would have lit only a very localised area. It is probably very difficult nowadays to appreciate the problems of moving quickly on foot in a shed yard in darkness. *A. Swain*

Below With its nameplates covered but in wonderful external condition, Derby 'Jubilee' No 45610 (formerly *Gold Coast*) is seen in the

shed yard at Willesden on 12 December 1958. Later that day, in a ceremony at Euston station, No 45610 was renamed *Ghana* by the Ghanaian High Commissioner in London to celebrate that country's independence.

Derby's 'Jubilees' worked to Leeds, Sheffield, Bristol, Bath and St Pancras in complicated diagrams and, as a boy, I would see *Gold Coast*, invariably dirty, regularly passing through Parkgate & Rawmarsh station on some part of such a duty. On 11 April 1955, as *Gold Coast*, it worked the 12.40 pm to Bristol out of Newcastle, the first time since 1949 that a 'Jubilee' had worked a regular service train out of that city. *A. Swain*

Above 'Coronation' Class 4-6-2 No 46220 *Coronation* at Willesden shed in March 1959. The 'Coronations' (the official LMS name for the Stanier 'Pacifics' that began to emerge from Crewe Works in 1937) worked principally on the West Coast Main Line services from Euston to Glasgow and Perth, and the Birmingham-Glasgow trains north of Crewe. When the English Electric Type 4 diesels arrived on the West Coast in 1959, their days were numbered, and by 1962 the 'Coronations' were seen increasingly on parcels and freight trains. They were regarded by many as perhaps the finest steam locomotives ever to run in Britain. *Coronation* herself was withdrawn in April 1963. *A. Swain*

Below Moving south of the Thames, this is a view of the front of the shed at Nine Elms on 4 September 1965, showing Standard Class '4' 2-6-4T No 80143, Standard Class '5' 4-6-0 No 73115 and Standard Class '4' 2-6-0 No 76053. Dominating the depot is the coaling plant with its concrete hoppers.

Although the last steam run to Waterloo was not to be until 9 July 1967, the feeling of a depot close to the end of its working life is unmistakeable in this photograph. Already weeds are growing beside and between tracks and there is an odd air of stillness where once men and engines would have been bustling. *A. Swain*

Left Rebuilt 'West Country' Class 4-6-2 No 34029 *Lundy* stands in the shed yard at Bristol Bath Road depot on 20 March 1960, having arrived earlier with an excursion from Portsmouth. The appearance of Bulleid 'Pacifics' in the Bristol area was noteworthy. On 13 November 1955, for example, 'BB' No 34090 *Sir Eustace Missenden, Southern Railway* was observed at Weston-super-Mare with an excursion from Brighton via Salisbury, possibly the first Southern Region engine to be seen there. 'West Country' Class No 34038 *Crediton* travelled to Ashton Gate with a football excursion in September 1958 and 'BB' 34051 *Winston Churchill* arrived at Temple Meads from Salisbury on 11 August 1962, and left piloting 'Hall' Class No 4960 *Pyle Hall* on the 10.50 am to Portsmouth Harbour. *D. J. Hucknall Collection*

Below 'Jubilee' Class 4-6-0 No 45699 *Galatea* stands over an ashpit at Canton depot, Cardiff. After fire-cleaning the smokebox will have been emptied of char - in this case, however, the job was incomplete since the buffer beam is covered with spilled char.

Galatea was at this time a Bristol (Barrow Road) engine and, until the summer of 1961, Bristol's 'Jubilees' were the principal motive power for the expresses linking Bristol, Newcastle, Bradford and Kingswear, such as the 'Devonian' and the Bristol-Newcastle and Derby-Bristol mail trains; they usually travelled through to Leeds or Sheffield. With the introduction of BR/Sulzer Type 4 2,500 hp diesels on the Bristol-Derby-Sheffield line, No 45699 and some of her sisters were redundant. In September 1961, *Galatea* (together with *Eire*, *Bengal*, *Shovell*, *Rooke* and *Leander*) was transferred to Shrewsbury. *H. G. Usmar*

The smoke from the chimney of 'Britannia' Class 4-6-2 No 70022 *Tornado* can almost be tasted in this shot of locomotives 'on shed' at Cardiff Canton. *Tornado* is standing by an ex-GWR standard 8-inch water crane, while in an adjacent siding stands '9F' Class 2-10-0 No 92231 and, further over, 'Britannia' Class No 70016 *Ariel*. Both of the 'Britannias' were transferred to Carlisle in the late summer of 1961 - *Ariel* went to Canal shed while *Tornado* was moved to Kingmoor.

Clearly shown are the hand holds cut into the smoke deflectors of *Tornado*. These replaced the handrails on the 'Britannias' which had been removed following criticism by the Inspecting Officer after the Milton accident of 22 November 1955. It was concluded that impairment of visibility by the handrails had contributed to the derailment of No 70026 *Polar Star* with loss of life. *H. G. Usmar*

Above There were probably few locomotives that would look small in comparison to an 'M7', but members of the ex-LSWR 'B4' Class most certainly did. Here, 'B4' No 30096 and 'M7' No 30375 are shown standing by the coal stack at the north end of Eastleigh shed.

The 'B4s' carried out various duties. One, No 30093, was allocated to Bournemouth for working on Poole quay. No 30096 was one of Eastleigh's engines and, together with No 30102, was the regular yard shunter and station pilot at Winchester City station. One of the pair would remain at Winchester for about a week and then return to Eastleigh for a boiler washout and servicing. Withdrawn in October 1963, No 30096 was sold to Corralls Ltd and worked at Dibles Wharf, Southampton, for a time. *D. J. Hucknall Collection*

Below Okehampton shed was a small one-road sub-depot of Exmouth Junction. It was made of concrete and erected by the LSWR after the original structure had burned down. No engines were allocated there but it was used for servicing and signing-on. Here 'Battle of Britain' Class 4-6-2 No 34083 *605 Squadron* (allocated to Exmouth Junction) stands in the shed entrance on 4 April 1964. The two-disc headcode was associated with a train travelling between Waterloo or Nine Elms and Plymouth. Okehampton was on the Southern route between Exeter and Plymouth. In the early 1950s there were six through services daily between Waterloo and Plymouth. The fastest time (5½ hours) was achieved by the 'Atlantic Coast Express', which nevertheless took 2 hrs 6 min between Exeter Central and Plymouth (Friary). The final trip of the 'ACE' was on 4 September 1964. *D. J. Hucknall*

Bournemouth mpd (71B) was a four-road shed located close to Central Station, and had quite a large allocation of locomotives. In the first week in November 1961, for example, this consisted of eight 'Merchant Navy' Class 'Pacifics', 18 'West Country/Battle of Britain' Class 4-6-2s, two 'N15' Class 4-6-0s, 13 'M7' Class 0-4-4Ts, three Class 'Q' 0-6-0Ts and seven BR Standard Class '4' 2-6-0s. The 'Merchant Navys' were used exclusively on Weymouth and Waterloo diagrams (and balancing local trips to get the locomotives down to Weymouth from the shed and back again). Bournemouth's 'WC/BB' 'Pacifics' could deputise

for the 'Merchant Navys', and also worked the 'Pines Express' to Bath over the Somerset & Dorset route. Another turn was the out-and-home trip to Oxford with trains such as the Bournemouth-York.

In this undated view of Bournemouth shed at least three 'West Country' Class locomotives can be seen. The unrebuilt locomotive is No 34008 *Padstow* (rebuilt, however, in mid-1960). To the left is No 34042 *Dorchester* (rebuilt around February 1959). The 'M7' on the right, No 30107, is standing by the locomotive hoist. *H. G. Usmar*

Left Holiday traffic to the 'Cornish Riviera' reached its peak in the late 1950s (see Alan Bennett's *The Great Western Railway in West Cornwall*). On summer Saturdays and Sundays the yard at Penzance shed at Long Rock would be full of locomotives. Rolling-stock would have been stored at Marazion, St Erth and even Gwinear Road, such was the shortage of space at Penzance.

This photograph, taken on 19 July 1959, shows a small section of the yard at 83G, filled with 'Halls' and 'Granges'. It was typical of this period, but thereafter the decline commenced; I returned four years later and things were very different. From left to right are Nos 7921 *Edstone Hall*, 6832 *Brockton Grange*, 7925 *Westol Hall* and 6988 *Swithland Hall*. Also on shed at the time, and noted down because I had never seen them before, were Nos 4908 (83G), 4913 (81D), 4976 (83D), 6802 (86G), 6824 (83G), 6845 (83G), 6855 (83G), 6863 (83D), 6871 (83D), 6911 (83G), 6913 (83D), 6931 (83E) and 7820 (83D). *D. J. Hucknall*

Below The line between Plymouth and Penzance was difficult for steam locomotives. It had sharp curves, laborious gradients, viaducts and dozens of cuttings and embankments. It was also a line that served the community with branches from Liskeard (for Looe), Bodmin Road (for Bodmin, Wadebridge and Padstow), Lostwithiel (for Fowey), Par (for Newquay), Truro (for Falmouth), Gwinear Road (for The Lizard, Cadgwith and Helston) and St Erth (for St Ives). As late as the 1950s regular pick-up trains ambled along the line, calling at all stations, collecting and delivering wagons.

'Prairie' tanks will always be synonymous with the Cornish branches and, on a Sunday afternoon in July 1959, Nos 4566 and 4564 stand at Penzance shed for servicing. I remember No 4566 as a regular on the Helston-Gwinear Road branch; it was also, almost exactly one year later, the last steam locomotive to be overhauled at Newton Abbot works. *D. J. Hucknall*

The first of the 'King' Class locomotives to be modified with a double blastpipe and double chimney was No 6015 *King Richard III* in the late summer/early autumn of 1955. The double-chimneyed 'Kings' were impressive-looking engines indeed. In my opinion, some of the finest photographs of the class at work were taken by David Fish who captured stunningly these fine locomotives blasting their way up Rattery and Dainton banks in spring and winter. I occasionally photographed 'Kings' passing Banbury with Birmingham trains but I had to wait some 30 years before I ever encountered one at very close quarters.

This photograph, taken at Didcot shed at noon on 9 June 1991, shows preserved No 6024 *King Edward I* in the process of being polished. *D. J. Hucknall*

Above A couple more preservation shots. Looking superb in the early morning sunshine at Ropley on 12 April 1987, 'Austerity' Class 2-10-0 No 90775 stands ready for duty on the Mid-Hants Railway. In all, 150 2-10-0s were built by North British Loco Co at its Hyde Park Works in Glasgow from 1943 to 1945, intended for use overseas by British Army personnel. A batch of 16 locomotives was sent to Egypt and there they remained in store.

At the end of 1948 the British Transport Commission bought 25 'Austerities' (Nos 90750-74) to work in the Scottish Region, but the locomotive numbered 90775 never formed part of British Railways' stock; it was one of the Egyptian 16. In 1946 the Hellenic State Railways acquired this batch, and the Mid-Hants Railway shipped what became No 90775 to England in 1981. *D. J. Hucknall*

Left Things may not always be as they seem with locomotives. An example from the 1930s was the 'Precursor' *Antaeus* which, after an error in Crewe Works, emerged with the name *Marquis*. The mistake was realised after a few days and eventually rectified. 'Castle' Class No 7013 *Bristol Castle* appeared as No 4082 *Windsor Castle* for King George VI's funeral train because the latter was in Swindon Works at the time; in this case their original identities were never restored. In September 1955 the Highland Light Infantry requested 'Royal Scot' Class No 46121 *Highland Light Infantry* to haul a troop train on 11 September. As 46121 was at Crewe Works at the time, its nameplates were transferred to sister engine 46123 *Royal Irish Fusilier*, which then carried out the duty.

This photograph, taken on Sunday 7 April 1991, appears to show 'BB' Class No 34067 *Tangmere* 'on shed' in ex-works condition. *Tangmere* is actually 'WC' Class *Swanage* standing at Ropley; the identity change was initially carried out as 'an April Fool's trick'. *D. J. Hucknall*

5. Portraits

Of course, it was always a stirring sight to see an express approaching, worked with full regulator and short cut-off with the driver concentrating on the road ahead, but for me the uniqueness and beauty of the steam locomotive could only be appreciated at close quarters.

It really was amazing that in a class of supposedly identical locomotives, each appeared to have its own character and idiosyncrasies. To read the experiences of men closely associated with engines and their running is to appreciate much more the enthusiasm that they had for their machines and the teamwork required to get the best out of them. Over the years, pen-portraits by railwaymen themselves revealed the 'character' of the steam locomotive; 'Toram Beg' (Norman McKillop), '45671' and Harold Gasson have written informatively and evocatively about their experiences.

'45671' (in *Trains Illustrated*, January 1958) on 'Black Fives' said 'That was a beautiful engine, No 45253. There was nothing that she could not do. . .', and 'All went well until a new batch of Class 5s, built in Horwich, were sent to Scotland and numbers 4796 and 4797 went to Perth. Right from the start they were in trouble.' Of the 'Jubilees' he said '. . .you do meet the black sheep among them, of course, and when you do . . . it is a devil of a job to get right - if you ever do succeed.'

Over the years some engines acquired good and bad reputations 'A1' No 60136 *Alcazar*, for instance, was a particularly rough-riding engine. No 60157 *Great Eastern* was fast, capable but ferocious at speed. Harold Gasson reported of the 'Castles' that No 5055 was the best in Old Oak Common, while No 5069 was the 'strongest'. Of the 'Kings', No 6014 was 'marvellous'. C. J. Allen records hearing 'A4' No 60011 described by a Perth driver as one of the finest engines he had been on in his life.

The practice, revived for a while in the immediate post-war years on certain parts of the railway system, of allocating an engine to one or two drivers led to care being lavished on certain engines so that they were in first-rate mechanical condition and performed accordingly. However, the introduction, initially on the LMS and later elsewhere, of the common-user locomotive led gradually to a deterioration in the appearance and condition of engines. There is a marvellous story in O. S. Nock's *Scottish Railways* (Nelson, 1961) concerning the 'A3' *Hyperion*. She was a real black sheep, 'wouldn't steam, wouldn't run, rode badly . . . in fact a thorough dud. . .' She had been a common-user engine, but Norman McKillop was given her while his regular engine was in the Plant. Nock quotes McKillop's words: 'Both of us spent a miserable week together. . . The following week was ideal, a run to Perth with Glenfarg to climb . . . a place to tell engines and men where the troubles lay.'

With the competent handling and expert diagnostic skills of McKillop, one by one *Hyperion*'s problems were eliminated until she '. . . slipped out of Edinburgh like a ghost, didn't seem to touch the rails at all on the level and kicked the mountains beneath her with contemptuous ease. . .'

Over the years many magnificent portraits of locomotives have been taken by renowned photographers, but in my opinion the best are on shed, at the end of a run, with, to quote Harold Gasson, 'the gloss of her deep Brunswick green filmed with dust and flattened flies. A gentle trickle of water dribbled from the injector water pipe, splashing quietly on to the charred sleepers.'

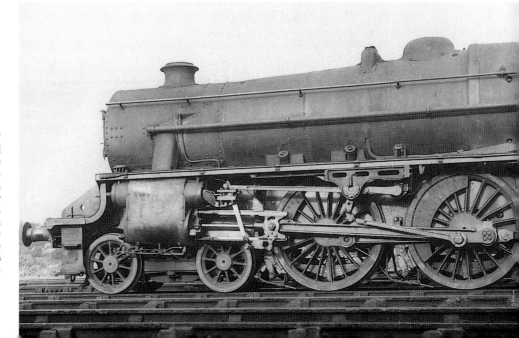

A photograph of an unidentified 'Black Five' taken at Perth shed shows in detail the standard Walschaerts motion of the Class. They were designed to be 'an engine that would go anywhere and do anything' (Rowledge and Reed in *The Stanier 4-6-0s*). '45671', a commentator whose articles on locomotive matters were both informative and highly readable, said of them (*Trains Illustrated*, January 1958), 'they were easy to fire and quite effective with a thick fire or a thin one, immune to fire-throwing unless grievously mishandled, steady on their feet - could a man want more?' *D. J. Hucknall*

Left Another 'Black Five' at Perth, No 45474, seen at close quarters. Clearly shown is the tablet-catching apparatus fitted to a good proportion of Scottish Class '5s'.

Carrying the power classification '5MT', the 'Black Fives' had a tractive effort of 25,455 lbs with an engine weight of $70\frac{1}{2}$ tons. The first of the Class, No 5020, appeared from Crewe Works in 1934. The initial order was for 70 engines, but eventually 842 were built. No 45474 entered service in May 1943 and was withdrawn 23 years later. *D. J. Hucknall*

Below The 'B1s' were the LNER's equivalent of the LMS's 'Black Fives' - fast engines, capable of long and heavy work. Although slightly more powerful than the Class '5s' (tractive effort 26,878 lbs at 85 per cent boiler pressure), they were never praised to the same extent, possibly because there were only half the number. Nevertheless, in the 1948 locomotive exchanges 'B1' No 61251 *Oliver Bury* destroyed the myth of the superiority of the 'Black Five'.

Withdrawals of the Class began in 1961 with Leicester's No 61085 (61057 had been scrapped earlier, having been damaged beyond repair in 1950). Even by 1966 almost 100 examples remained. Here, seen in early March 1965, one of 64A's 'B1s', No 61099, stands outside Dundee (Tay Bridge) shed. She was eventually withdrawn from Thornton Junction in November 1966 and was scrapped at Faslane in the following month. *D. J. Hucknall*

'Black Five' No 45473 rests in Perth shed on 27 June 1965, strikingly illuminated by the lowering evening sun. The quietness of the Sunday evening was only disturbed by the gentle hiss of steam and the occasional footplate noises elsewhere in the shed. *D. J. Hucknall*

'Britannia' Class No 70036 (formerly *Boadicea*) entered service at Stratford shed in December 1952, was transferred to Norwich in January 1959 and to Immingham in September 1961. During December 1963 several 'Britannias' were transferred from the Eastern Region to Carlisle Kingmoor and Upperby; No 70036 went to 12A in March 1964. Some of them were in poor condition and it was not until the fol-lowing summer that they began to appear regularly on passenger trains.

Here, close to the end of her working days, No 70036 stands outside Perth shed on 24 April 1965. Gone are the days on the Great Eastern line when, in pristine condition, she and her sisters rejuvenated the services from Liverpool Street to and from East Anglia. Instead, increasingly begrimed, they helped with duties north of Carlisle as substitutes for diesels. *D. J. Hucknall*

Above From June 1937 until its transfer to Ferryhill some 25 years later, 'A4' Class No 60009 *Union of South Africa* was a Haymarket engine. In the 1950s she was a consistent performer on the most demanding of East Coast expresses such as the 'Capitals Limited' and its successor the 'Elizabethan'. During the summer of 1954 No 60009 worked the latter in two long spells (it appeared almost daily between early August and mid-September). As schoolboys at the time, my friends and I would cycle to Doncaster and from the vantage point of St James's Bridge would regularly see No 60009, beautifully cleaned, easing through the station at a steady 50-60 mph. Occasionally, we would see steam from its whistle form a bow wave on either side of the chimney just before its long, haunting note could be heard.

In their later years several 'A4s' were transferred to 61B to work the 3-hour trains between Glasgow and Aberdeen. Perth men, who worked them between Perth and Glasgow, had a high regard for No 60009 and her sister No 60011. Of the latter, it was reported (by C. J. Allen, *Modern Railways*, December 1962) that one 63A driver looked on her as the finest engine he had ever been on in his life. When No 60009 emerged from the Works in December 1963, she was to be the last steam locomotive to be overhauled at Doncaster.

No longer in quite such pristine condition, but still a capable engine, *Union of South Africa* is shown in this photograph at Perth shed in the spring of 1965. Withdrawn in June 1966, she was sold to J. B. Cameron one month later for preservation. *D. J. Hucknall*

Right Locomotives on their way to and from Inverurie Works would use Ferryhill shed, Aberdeen. In this photograph, taken on a brilliantly sunny but icily cold afternoon in early March 1965, one of Thornton's 'J37' Class 0-6-0s, No 64569, stands in the yard at 61B after a general overhaul. Inverurie also dealt with a few English locomotives. The first was Gateshead's 'J39' No 64704, overhauled during April/May 1960. *D. J. Hucknall*

Above Lowering clouds on 17 April herald yet another miserable day in the spring of 1965. Outside St Margarets shed are 'A4' Class No 60006 *Sir Ralph Wedgwood* and a 'B1'. On shed at the time were 'A4' No 60027 *Merlin*, 'V2s' Nos 60813 and 60816 and various 'B1s' and BR Standard 2-6-0s. The original *Sir Ralph Wedgwood* (No 4466) had been destroyed during an air raid on York, and No 4466 *Herring Gull* was renamed. Sent to Scotland from the Eastern Region at the end of October 1963, she emerged from store at Dalry Road on 13 May 1964 and was then sent to Aberdeen. *D. J. Hucknall*

Left An extremely dirty 'A3' Class 4-6-2 No 60100 *Spearmint* stands in the yard at St Margarets in early 1965 - I never saw *Spearmint* in any other state. Some 13 years earlier, in the late summer of 1952, I had cycled to Doncaster and had seen her on shed prior to entering the locomotive works. As would be expected, she was filthy, but under the grime the blue livery, applied at an earlier works visit, was just visible. *Spearmint* spent the greater portion of her life (May 1930-April 1937; March-July 1938; December 1940-January 1963) allocated to Haymarket shed in Edinburgh, and was assigned to driver Norman McKillop. In one of his books, Charles Meacher states that McKillop had his fireplace decorated with a nameplate from *Spearmint* but that Mrs McKillop persuaded him 'to get rid of it'. No 60100 entered Darlington Works for repair in May 1965 but was condemned on 19 June and cut up. *D. J. Hucknall*

Right The 'V2s' were good-looking engines, and when they were fitted with outside steam pipes, they were very much in the tradition of the 'A3s'. The first example of the Class appeared in 1936 and an article in the *Engineer* of that year suggested that the 'V2' was the most powerful locomotive on 10 wheels in Britain at that time. (J. F. Clay, 'The V2s' in *Essays in Steam*). They were very well received in Scotland, and Dundee's No 60836 looks particularly competent and striking as it stands outside St Margaret's shed. In summarising the work of the Class, John Clay pointed out that they had been a national asset before and during the Second World War but were less successful in the post-war conditions. 'There was, perhaps,' he said, 'too much racehorse blood in the "V2s" to make them successful hacks'. *D. J. Hucknall*

Below No 60052 *Prince Palatine*, converted from Gresley's 'A1' Class in August 1941, stands outside St Margarets on 7 February 1965, having been transferred there in late August 1963 from Gateshead. Clearly visible are the vacuum ejector exhaust pipe along the side of the boiler and the reversing rod below the running plate. No 60052 was eventually withdrawn on 17 January 1966, and stood outside the shed at St Margarets for some time afterwards before being sold for scrap in the following June. *D. J. Hucknall*

Below right I have never tired of looking at locomotive nameplates - some were so appropriate to the engines and their duties. The 'A3s' and 'A2s', for example, were named after the winners of classic horse races, which seemed very apt for locomotives that dashed the length of the East Coast Main line from King's Cross to Edinburgh.

A close-up of the nameplate of *Prince Palatine* reveals clearly every detail - each blemish and stain on the locomotive, from the corroded patches on the top surface of the boiler down to the grease and grime on the connecting rods and wheel spokes. *D. J. Hucknall*

Above 'A3' Class No 60051 *Blink Bonny* first entered service with the LNER as an 'A10', but was rebuilt in November 1945. For a few years, in the mid-1950s, she worked from Copley Hill shed (May 1954-Sept 1957), dashing up and down the East Coast Main Line on that shed's turns (the up 'White Rose', 'Queen of Scots', the 7.50 am down from King's Cross, etc).

From September 1957 until her condemnation in November 1964, she was sent to the North East, mainly allocated to either Gateshead or Darlington sheds. In this photograph, taken on 2 May 1964, No 60051 is seen outside York mpd. Because she was working a special she had been embellished with silver-painted hinge-straps on the smokebox door. *D. J. Hucknall*

Right By contrast, simmering in the August sunshine at Cambridge shed in 1958 is 'J15' No 65477. Built in August 1913 and with her 4 ft 11 in wheels and tall chimney, she gives the impression of an engine capable only of pottering about with a few wagons on some straggling branch. In fact, the Class carried out some very hard work indeed in pre-Grouping days, hauling loaded coal trains from March to Temple Mills. At the Grouping 272 'J15s' passed to the LNER, but in the 1950s their elimination was rapid. No 65477 lasted until February 1960. *W. A. C. Smith*

Left The rebuilt Bulleid 4-6-2s were, in my opinion, very handsome locomotives, and this shot of 'West Country' Class No 34098 *Templecombe* taken at Banbury mpd on 2 January 1966 hardly does the Class justice. It is noteworthy, however, because it was one of the few presentable locomotives on the shed that day. The three ex-GWR engines (Nos 6916 *Misterton Hall*, 6930 *Aldersey Hall* and 7912 *Little Linford Hall*) also there were dreadfully dilapidated with the matt grey-brown colour that resulted from prolonged and deliberate neglect. Only a few years earlier I had been delighted by the 'Halls' at Banbury, and the dereliction of the three shocked and annoyed me. Banbury shed was closed almost exactly nine months after this photograph was taken. *D. J. Hucknall*

Right In happier days, on 8 August 1958, 'Grange' Class 4-6-0 No 6848 *Toddington Grange* stands at Banbury shed. Banbury received three brand new 'Granges' (Nos 6839/43/44) in 1937 and by 1944 eight of the Class (Nos 6803/16/32/35/39/41/49/54) were stationed there. As the importance of the shed gradually declined, its allocation fell steadily and the 'Granges' had gone by the early 1950s. According to P. B. Hands (*BR Steam Shed Allocations*, Pt 1 Western Region Sheds), No 6848 was a Laira engine until September 1958 when it was transferred to Oxford. *D. J. Hucknall*

Below A portrait of 'Castle' Class No 7020 *Gloucester Castle* (81A) at Oxford shed; one of a group of post-war 'Castles' (Nos 5098/99, 7000-07 were completed by the Great Western Railway by July 1946), No 7020 was built by British Railways in the first half of 1949. It remained in its original condition until 1961 when it was fitted with a double chimney and blastpipe. It was transferred to 81A from Cardiff Canton at the beginning of 1957 and remained there until June 1964. It was withdrawn from Southall shed in September 1964. *D. J. Hucknall Collection*

Left A rather grimy 'Castle', No 5092 *Tresco Abbey* (an 82A engine from April 1958 to August 1960), stands in the shed yard at Bristol Bath Road. Clearly visible on the left-hand side of the smokebox, ahead of the outside steampipe, is the mechanical lubricator designed to deliver a pre-set feed of oil to the cylinders and valves. On the right-hand side of the buffer beam is a rag, a can of paraffin and a flare lamp. Rather crudely chalked on the smokebox door is the train reporting number, 433 - this used to be associated with the 6.40 am Leicester-Paignton train. *H. G. Usmar*

Below Another Bath Road 'Castle' study, this time No 5069 *Isambard Kingdom Brunel* by the side of the coaling stage. This stage was 90 feet long and had three coal tips, while the tank above it held 135,000 gallons of water, pumped from the River Avon at Foxes Wood via a 15-inch diameter pipe.

This time the train reporting number is displayed in a metal frame carried on the smokebox door, as was the practice during the 1950s on certain passenger trains. I have not been able to identify the number 212 unambiguously; no such number is reported in the winter lists for 1956/7 or 1957/8, although from Whitehouse and Jenkinson (*From BR to Beeching*, Vol 1, Atlantic Transport Publishers 1990), train 212 appears to have been the summer 9.10 am Manchester (London Road) to Paignton. According to these authors the WR worked it from Bristol onwards and the sheds involved were usually 82A or Newton Abbot (83A). I have a photograph, however, showing a 'Castle' with '212' on the smokebox door at Reading (General) station. *H. G. Usmar*

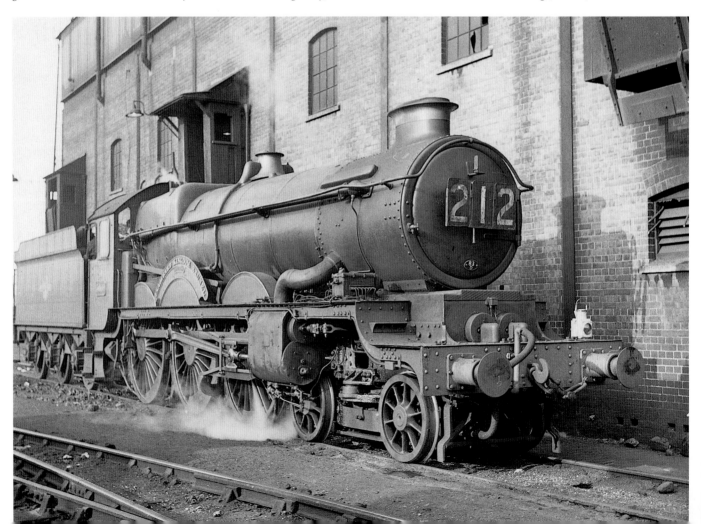

Another wonderfully evocative picture of *Isambard Kingdom Brunel* at Bath Road. At this time she was a Laira engine; in 1952 she had been transferred to Bath Road from Old Oak Common in exchange for Bristol's solitary 'King', No 6000 *King George V*.

During the 1950s lightly loaded boat trains were run from Millbay Docks, Plymouth, to Paddington. On 7 October 1954 No 5069, with Driver Hammett and Fireman Luscombe in charge, set a then record time of 3 hrs 37 min to Paddington with a train of five coaches (171 tons tare). No 5069's performance was later equalled (20 October 1954) by No 5058 *Earl of Clancarty* with seven vehicles. *H. G. Usmar*

Seen with pin-point definition at Willesden shed on 11 June 1961 is 'Jubilee' No 45672 *Anson*. Her allocation (1A at this time) is painted on the smokebox door. *Anson* appeared to be a locomotive that was transferred with surprising regularity. She was allocated to Bushbury in late February 1957, Camden in late November of the same year and went to Upperby shed, Carlisle, on 4 October 1958. She was transferred to Willesden at the beginning of March 1961.

In 1964 *Anson* had the dubious distinction of spending a great deal of unplanned time on the Southern Region. Arriving at Eastbourne shed on 19 June, she was used the following day on a local working to Haywards Heath. Later on the 20th she failed on the Newhaven-Glasgow car-sleeper. After being dumped on Brighton shed in the early hours of the 21st, she was eventually released on 2 July and returned slowly, light engine, to Willesden. *A. Swain*

Above Another Willesden view, this time of Leicester 'Black Five' No 45264 on 27 April 1963, rostered for 1T05 (a Wembley to Melton Mowbray train). As has already been mentioned, the writer '45671' wrote of the wonderful reputation of the 'Black Fives' with LM enginemen. He pointed out that they were simple machines, easy to fire and to service, comfortable to ride on and capable of tackling most work. He had travelled regularly on the pre-war 4.30 pm from Manchester Central, the seven to eight coach train being increased at Derby by a further three coaches and several loaded 3,000-gallon milk tanks. 'Out of Loughborough' he reminisced, 'on that gentle but dragging 1 in 508 . . . No 5264 or one of her sisters would be sent storming away and would have that big train well into the sixties before the Leicester stop.' A. Swain

Right Brand new, Standard Class '4MT' 2-6-4T No 80099 went to Plaistow to work on the London, Tilbury & Southend line. In November 1959 she was transferred to Tilbury, where she stayed until June 1962. Eventually reaching Machynlleth shed in July 1963, she spent the rest of her days working the beautiful lines of the former Cambrian Railways. Photographed at Aberystwyth shed, No 80099 still looks impressive. Although its lined-out livery is rather drab and dirty, against the foothills of Snowdonia or the wild saltings of the Dovey estuary it would still be a stirring sight. D. J. Hucknall Collection

Above left Rebuilt 'West Country' Class 'Pacific' No 34022 *Exmoor* and BR Standard Class '4' 4-6-0 No 75077 stand at Eastleigh. One of the fascinations about Eastleigh was the procession of engines bound for the Works. Reference to journals such as the *Railway Observer* shows that in the period 7 September to 5 October 1963, 36 locomotives arrived for attention, including five 'WC/BB' 'Pacifics'. One year later, from 3 August to 12 September, the tally was 38 locomotives, including three 'light Pacifics' and two 'Merchant Navys'.

Normally, an engine had a general or intermediate repair every 2-2½ years, the general repair involving a complete strip-down, including boiler removal. An intermediate involved stripping down the engine with the boiler in position. *H. G. Usmar*

Left Also at Eastleigh, 'Lord Nelson' Class 4-6-0 No 30850 *Lord Nelson* stands outside the shed. Towards the end of their careers, all the 'Nelsons' were allocated to 71A. Designed by R. E. L. Maunsell, the first of the Class was introduced in 1926. They were erratic performers, however, until Oliver Bulleid redesigned the front ends and gave them new cylinders, Lemaitre multiple-jet blastpipes and a large diameter chimney. Their performance improved dramatically but they were displaced from primary mainline duties by Bulleid's 'Pacifics'. Jim Evans, who had fired on the

'Nelsons', said of them, '. . . the Lord Nelsons were the complete steam locomotive. . . At speed the footplate set so high and far behind the rear wheel would roll at amazing angles, a sensation that would make the blood pound with excitement.' *D. J. Hucknall Collection*

Above Although renowned for their free-steaming and the consistency of the work they produced, Bulleid's 'Pacifics', as originally designed, were highly controversial engines. Externally, the air-smoothed casing over the whole of the upper part of the locomotive was unusual, but other features, such as the oil bath that enclosed the valve gear, proved troublesome and costly from the point of view of maintenance and accessibility.

To overcome these problems, the whole of the 'Merchant Navy' Class and a number of the 'West Country/Battle of Britain' Class were rebuilt with, among many features, an orthodox cylindrical smokebox, outside valve gear and large smoke deflectors. The result was a very impressive-looking locomotive as is clearly shown in this photograph of 'West Country' Class No 34097 *Holsworthy*, taken at Eastleigh in the 1960s. No 34097 had been a Brighton engine, moving to Exmouth Junction in November 1960. She was one of the final batch of 30 locomotives to be rebuilt in early 1961. *H. G. Usmar*

Left Okehampton shed, a sub-depot of Exmouth Junction, was a one-road building located at the Exeter end of Okehampton station on the ex-SR route from Plymouth to Exeter; the station was sited on a hillside above the town which clustered in the Okement valley. Here we see 'N' Class 2-6-0 No 31834 standing in the shed yard on the morning of 4 April 1964. It was quite an unpleasant day and shortly after the shot was taken a sleet storm swept down from the hills with an intensity that made further photography pointless. *D. J. Hucknall*

Below left St Blazey's 'Manor' Class 4-6-0 No 7816 *Frilsham Manor* stands in the yard at Penzance shed, Long Rock (83G), on 12 August 1957. In the South West 'Manors' were used extensively on pilot duties; by the summer of 1960, however, all passenger and parcel trains between Penzance and Plymouth were diesel-powered. A regular 'Manor' duty that remained involved piloting the 8.55 am (SO) Wolverhampton to Newquay and Penzance service from Plymouth to Par. On 2 July 1960 No 7816 was involved in triple-heading the train from Plymouth.

No 7816 left St Blazey in September 1960 and was transferred to Tyseley, being later drafted to Reading (September 1962-August 1964). There, on 17 June 1963, whilst acting as station pilot, she had to take over the 1.50 pm from Penzance after the failure of the rostered diesel, 'Warship' Class No D836 *Powerful*. *D. J. Hucknall*

Right It is not difficult to understand the considerable pleasure that the locomotives of the former Great Western Railway have given to the railway enthusiasts of Britain, being associated in the minds of many with sunny childhood summers spent in Cornwall or Devon. This photograph of 'County' Class 4-6-0 No 1006 *County of Cornwall* was taken on 12 August 1957 at Penzance mpd when I was 16 years old. The afternoon sun shone on the copper band of the chimney and highlighted the 6 ft 3 in driving wheels, while the air had the 'summer' railway smell of creosoted sleepers and warm oil and metal mixed with salty sea breezes. *D. J. Hucknall*

Above Reflected in the polished paintwork of 'Warship' Class No D841 *Roebuck* on 11 July 1965 are the windows of the former steam depot at Penzance. For 13 years the shed carried the code 83G, but in late 1963 the Western Region's motive power depots in the area were recoded - Laira became 84A, St Blazey 84B, Truro 84C and Penzance 84D. *D. J. Hucknall*

Right Newton Abbot's 'Castle' No 4077 *Chepstow Castle* stands in the yard at Penzance on 19 July 1959. To her right 'Modified Hall' No 7921 *Edstone Hall* can be seen. At the time, 83G's allocation included four 'County' 4-6-0s, two 'Castles' (*Harlech Castle* and *Trematon Castle*), four 'Halls', one 'Modified Hall' and 14 'Granges'.

On a summer Saturday in the 1950s the shed and yard would be full of 'Halls' and 'Granges'. For example, on the day of this photograph among the locos in the yard were Nos 6824 *Ashley Grange*, 6832 *Brockton Hall*, 6913 *Levens Hall*, 6988 *Swithland Hall*, 7925 *Westol Hall*, 6911 *Holker Hall*, 6931 *Aldborough Hall* and 4908 *Broome Hall*. *D. J. Hucknall*

Left Steam portraits take on a new perspective in the preservation era. Here the feeble morning sun emphasises the beautiful finish on Urie 'S15' Class No 30506. Repainted in unlined black, the mirror-like gloss reflects the branches of the trees next to the sidings as she stands outside the works/shed at Ropley on the Mid-Hants line on 6 February 1993.

Built at Eastleigh in October 1920, as No 506 she was initially allocated to Nine Elms, working heavy goods trains to and from Southampton Docks, Eastleigh, Salisbury and Exmouth Junction. By mid-1928 she was at Feltham where the work involved freights to Reading, Willesden, Dorchester and other destinations. She and her sisters also hauled relief passenger trains to Bournemouth, Salisbury, etc. In the summer immediately before withdrawal, she regularly appeared on the 6.37 am Basingstoke-Waterloo.

No 30506 was withdrawn in January 1964 having covered 1,227,897 miles. In June of that year she towed Nos 30499/841/7 to Woodham Bros scrapyard in Barry, where she lay rusting until bought by the Urie 'S15' Preservation Society and delivered to the Mid-Hants Railway in November 1983. *D. J. Hucknall*

Below A close-up of 'Britannia' Class 4-6-2 No 70000 *Britannia*, photographed at Ropley two days later on 8 February 1993, a day of incredible dullness and gloom. The 'Britannias', including No 70000, appeared on the Great Eastern section from 1951 onwards, and eventually some 23 locomotives were allocated between Stratford (13) and Norwich (10) sheds.

Britannia herself was a Stratford engine and when involved on that shed's No 9 turn (boat trains to and from Parkeston Quay) she was always splendidly clean and in tip-top mechanical condition. Behind No 70000 can be seen part of the Urie 5,000-gallon tender fitted to No 30506, which, until September 1956, had belonged to 'N15' No 30745 *Tintagel*. *D. J. Hucknall*

The date is 28 May 1990 and, beautiful and burnished, 'King' Class No 6024 *King Edward I* pauses in its duties at Didcot to replenish its tender with water, a reminder of the heyday of steam locomotive operation in Britain. The pride with which the driver is describing his locomotive to an admiring audience can well be imagined.

The 'Kings' used to be responsible for the heaviest, fastest duties on the Western Region. O. S. Nock (*British Railways in Action*, Nelson 1956) describes brilliantly the impression of a 'King' at speed: '. . . to see and hear the "Bristolian" approach and pass is an experience not to be readily forgotten. With the up express at 85 to 90 mph the exhaust beat is just loud enough to be distinguished; there is usually a faint "tick-tick-tick-tick-tick" from the cylinder relief valves. The sensation of speed is tremendous.' *D. J. Hucknall*

6. Interlude: Trainspotters

I now realise that I was not much of a trainspotter. Looking once again through my old 'Combineds' (*Ian Allan ABC of British Railways Locomotives*, Combined Edition), I can see whole classes of locomotives where only a handful of the engines are marked off. I did, however, manage to see all the 'A1s' and 'A4s', but four 'A3s' (Nos 60074/87/99/111) evaded me - this in spite of living only 12 miles from Doncaster and spending hours sitting on wooden fences beside the East Coast Main Line at Bawtry and Ranskill. I fared little better with the 'Jubilees' - No 45552 and the Scottish engines rarely ran through Rotherham.

I suppose I lacked dedication. I was just not prepared to trek around the country, clambering over walls covered with broken glass, dashing for the cover of wagons and generally running the gauntlet of the railway authorities.

One drawback to lineside spotting was that it seemed to take an awfully long time to accumulate numbers, while sheds provided the opportunity to get them very quickly. Unfortunately, the same engines were always on the local sheds. Nevertheless, I would return time after time in the perpetual hope that a rare engine, particularly a 'namer', would be lurking among the usual tired-looking, uninspiring 'WDs', '8Fs' and '4Fs' of a freight-only depot like Canklow. Throughout my railway days I never lost that feeling of anticipation as I approached a shed. It was for this reason that I used to enjoy Perth so much - and my expectations were usually fulfilled.

One solution to the dedicated locospotter's perennial problem of seeing every locomotive in Britain was to join one of the Locospotters Clubs that were so active in the 1950s and early '60s. Announcements of their activities would appear in magazines like *Trains Illustrated* - whirlwind tours of all the sheds in cities such as Birmingham, Manchester and Liverpool, or marathons covering swathes of the country. Peter Hands (see *Chasing Steam on Shed*, Barbryn Press Ltd 1982) chronicles his travels with the Railway Enthusiasts Club based in Birmingham, including a two-day trip to the North East of England in February (!) 1962 - '19 sheds visited,' he reported, '796 steam and 174 diesels seen, all for 55 shillings.'

The exploits of the serious trainspotter seem bewildering - dashes around Gateshead or Tebay sheds in the dead of night, for example. As Peter Hands recalls, '. . . we made an attempt to bunk Kingmoor in the dark but whilst in the shed yard we were warned by a driver that the police were present and so we gave up. . .'

In spite of my more tentative approach to the hobby, I had some marvellous times. Shed foremen at places such as Penzance and Banbury could be very understanding, and I shall always remember leisurely strolls around depots, taking the occasional photograph. My father used to be a keen bowls player, and once I travelled with the team to Wakefield for a match. The bowling green must have been very close to Wakefield mpd because I spent a long, sunny afternoon watching a seemingly endless parade of previously unseen locomotives (predominantly 'Austerities') trundle on and off the shed.

The afternoon drew to a perfect close, for just before I left I noticed the setting sun glinting on the burnished boiler of an approaching engine. As it drew nearer I could see that it was a 'Jubilee' (No 45717 from Bank Hall, in fact). It was a magnificent sight - an engine I had never seen before gliding past me, her piston rods gleaming in the last of the light.

York mpd on Saturday 2 May 1964 - with his gabardine raincoat (almost a uniform for the railway enthusiast of the period) sensibly belted, a trainspotter strolls past Worsdell 'J27' Class 0-6-0 No 65844, notebook in hand. For the railwayman striding purposefully in the opposite direction it was just another working day. *D. J. Hucknall*

A delighted boy gazes at the nameplate of 'Castle' Class 4-6-0 No 7018 *Drysllwyn Castle*. Railway sheds were wonderful because they presented an opportunity to see such outstanding locomotives at very close quarters indeed. It never seemed to be understood by the chroniclers that, as schoolboys, very few of us really had any appreciation of the mechanical aspects of railway engines, nor of the superb achievements of their crews. We would, however, travel miles to look at a 'rare' locomotive and underline it in our lists, and most of us can understand the feelings of this boy.

Previously an indifferent steamer, No 7018 had a double blastpipe and chimney fitted after which its performance was transformed. On one occasion, heading the up 'Bristolian' with Driver Russe (82A) in charge, No 7018 shifted a seven-coach train (260 tons gross) with, according to C. J. Allen (*Trains Illustrated*, September 1958), 'phenomenal' acceleration from Badminton to Wootton Bassett. He estimated that 102 mph 'at least' was reached at Little Somerford. *D. J. Hucknall Collection*

Above Steam sheds acted as magnets for trainspotters. According to the rules, visits to sheds had to be arranged officially and with some of the larger ex-LMS and ex-LNER depots, this was the only way. It would have been the very faint-hearted, however, who would not have used a convenient wall or attempted to sneak past the shed office to find a much sought-after engine. Sometimes the shed superintendent and his staff could be very understanding, and Sundays were excellent days for an unofficial look around.

Two very young men are seen here on the right patrolling the shed at Plymouth Laira (83D). Dominating the picture, however, is 'County' Class No 1006 *County of Cornwall*. She had been transferred to 83D in October 1960 after a brief period (May-October) at St Blazey and remained there until December 1962. By this time fitted with a double chimney, No 1006 lacked some of its original appeal (see elsewhere in this book). *H. G. Usmar*

Left 'Castle' Class 4-6-0 No 5092 *Tresco Abbey* (82A, Bristol Bath Road) comes under scrutiny from a more mature enthusiast. No 5092 was transferred to 82A in April 1958 from Reading shed (81D) as part of a re-shuffle in the allocations of 32 'Castles' among 13 depots which was aimed at dispersing high-mileage locos throughout the Western Region. Joining No 5092 at the time were No 5015 *Kingswear Castle*, No 5073 *Blenheim* and No 5090 *Neath Abbey*. *D. J. Hucknall Collection*

7. Repairs

Repairs, often major ones, were part of the continuous struggle at a motive power depot to find enough engines to fulfil the allotted duties. Failures in service could cause great delay and inconvenience. In an awful period from mid-September 1953 to May 1954 King's Cross shed had, on average, one failure every 3½ days, with its 'A4s', 'A3s' and 'V2s'. Seventeen failures occurred with the 'Tees-Tyne Pullman' alone.

Some sheds were large enough and regarded as sufficiently important to have extensive facilities. Lathes, presses, wheel-drops, overhead cranes, forges, etc, were all available in these depots, and quite major repairs were carried out. At 'A' sheds such as Perth and Exmouth Junction, conditions were good - the repair shops were light and airy with appropriate equipment. Generally, however, there seemed to be no pattern - Oxford (81F) and Didcot (81E) had repair shops, while a main shed such as St Margarets had scant facilities. Alec Swain's photograph (page 117) of No 60004 at Haymarket with piston rings hanging from the buffers shows that even first-line depots had to cope with very basic conditions.

Maintenance work on locomotives could range from routine boiler washouts, valve and piston examinations to superheater repairs, hot axle-box correction and wheel-turning. Repairs could be carried out in the running shed, but usually this was needed for washouts. It was not uncommon at some sheds to see a locomotive in the yard jacked up on timbers, minus coupling-rods and surrounded by the usual fitter's paraphernalia - hammers, spanners, oxy-acetylene cylinders.

Richard Hardy (in *Steam in the Blood*, Ian Allan 1971) describes the primitive conditions that prevailed at some sheds. At Ipswich in the 1950s he recalls valve and piston examinations being carried out '. . . in the teeth of the easterly gales that blew straight in from the North Sea'. Describing Stewarts Lane main shed, he comments 'It was dark, ill-lit and low in the roof, and it was here that all the heavy repairs, washing out and servicing was carried out,' It must have been a great burden and perpetual headache to fitters and foremen to maintain skill and care under such conditions, for just one mistake could be costly, resulting in failure or accident.

At Crewe North the examination and repair shed, completed in 1959, was designed to provide all the facilities for specialist work on the ex-LMS 'Pacifics'. It was commandeered, however, as Crewe Diesel Depot, allegedly without seeing a single steam engine.

Although 'A4s' were frequent visitors to the depot (on 14 March 1959, for example, four of Haymarket's 'A4s', Nos 60009/11/27/31, were on shed simultaneously), Aberdeen Ferryhill did not have any of its own until 1962. During the period 1962-66, however, 11 'A4s' (60004/6/9/10/11/12/16/19/23/24 and 34) were allocated there at various times. They covered most passenger trains between Glasgow and Aberdeen (the exception was the 9.30 am) and also express freight trains on both the East Coast route to Edinburgh and on the route leading to the West Coast.

Latterly a 61B engine, 'A4' No 60004 *William Whitelaw* is shown standing outside the repair and machine stop at Ferryhill on 6 March 1965. Access to the smokebox of the 'A4s' was via the oddly named 'cod's mouth'. The bottom section was let down and held by chains (just discernible in the photograph) while the upper door was operated by a crank inserted below the front part of the running plate. *D. J. Hucknall*

Left Early in March 1965 I was visiting Perth mpd, and inside the shed was 'A4' No 60010 *Dominion of Canada*. I mentioned to a passing railwayman that it was a pity that it was not outside. With the kindness that was typical of many enginemen, No 60010 was duly brought out so that I could photograph her. Looking now at the stained leading driving wheel and valve gear, she must have failed while working a train earlier in the day.

By that date No 60010 was an Aberdeen engine, having been transferred there on 20 October 1963 after a period in store. From May 1937 until April 1957 and from 15 September 1957 until 6 June 1963 she had been a King's Cross engine. While there, on 3 June 1937 as No 4489, she achieved speeds of between $102\frac{1}{2}$ and $109\frac{1}{2}$ mph between Little Bytham and Essendine. *D. J. Hucknall*

Below Perth shed had some impressive repair facilities. Following the tradition of the Caledonian Railway, these were situated beside the engine shed, but with the stores, machine shop, etc between. Here one of 63A's own 'Black Fives', No 44799, is undergoing examination. The photograph was taken on 27 June 1965 and may record the end of the line for the engine; she was withdrawn in July. *D. J. Hucknall*

Engineering work in and around engine sheds was sometimes carried out with fairly makeshift equipment. It was not unusual to see cranes and pulleys attached to wooden posts lashed to running plates and buffer beams. In this photograph, taken at Ladyburn shed, Greenock, in September 1956, ex-Caledonian Railway 0-4-4T No 55267 and 4-4-0 No 54456 are providing power for a compressor and a small crane being used to repair the turntable.

Ladyburn was an old shed, opened by the Caledonian Railway in 1884. In 1959 it had 39 engines, but by 1965 this had fallen to 12 and the shed eventually closed in December 1966. *W. A. C. Smith*

Above Ex-NBR Class 'J36' No 65234, being prepared for duty as a stationary boiler on the site of the old roundhouse at St Margarets on 7 February 1965; on the right is the usual style of stationary boiler mounted on a permanent base. Like the locomotive, the equipment used to carry out the work is a relic of railway practice at the beginning of the century. It consists of a spar carrying block and tackle and crudely lashed to the hand-rails, running-plate and spokes of the centre driving wheel. *D. J. Hucknall*

Left Looking at shabby 'V2' Class No 60846 standing in St Margarets shed in 1965, it was easy to forget the years of excellent work that the Class had completed. In July 1939, as No 4817, based at Doncaster, No 60846 made a very good run to London with the 'Yorkshire Pullman'. She covered the 156 miles from Doncaster to King's Cross in 151 min 44 sec, including three signal stops. The 17.6 miles from Corby to Werrington were covered at an average speed of 86.2 mph, while the average for the 9.4 miles from Little Bytham to Tallington was 90.2 mph; the top speed was 93 mph.

Later in her career she was based in the North East of England (Ardsley, Heaton and Thornaby), but was transferred to St Margarets in March 1963. At the end of the summer of 1965 she was one of three 64A 'V2s' that were withdrawn. After two months in store she was scrapped at Airdrie in January 1966. *D. J. Hucknall*

Above Slanting through a skylight, shafts of sun penetrate the gloom of St Margarets and illuminate 'V2' No 60846 undergoing repairs. Attached to her right-hand front lamp bracket is a 'Not to be moved' sign and the gas bottles by the buffers suggest that the fitters are not far away. At the beginning of 1965, when this photograph was taken, 64A had eight 'V2s'. They found regular work on Edinburgh to Perth passenger trains and were frequently used on goods trains on the Waverley route to Carlisle. *D. J. Hucknall*

Below Two of Haymarket's 'Pacifics', 'A4' Class No 60004 *William Whitelaw* and 'A1' Class No 60161 *North British* at Haymarket shed on Sunday 6 September 1959 - both are obviously out of action. No 60004 is undergoing an examination of its pistons and valves in the open; the piston and valve rings are hanging from the lamp brackets. Alec Swain, who took the photograph and who had been Chief Mechanical Foreman at Leicester shed, comments 'I would not have expected my fitters to work under those conditions.' *A. Swain*

Left Standing dramatically in the doorway of Canklow shed is Holbeck's 'Black Five' No 45273. It was the spring of 1965 and Canklow was in its final year of operation as a steam shed. When I first visited it as a boy, Johnson Midland '2F' 0-6-0s were still in operation and a visit from a 'Black Five' would have been rare indeed. Canklow was to stand empty for another 15 years after this photograph was taken before demolition. *D. J. Hucknall*

Above Inside No 2 shed at Wellingborough on 29 April 1962 stands little ex-Midland Railway Johnson Class '2F' No 58148 from Coalville shed. She is receiving attention to her cylinders and valves prior to working a special railtour over the branch line from West Bridge, Leicester, to Desford Junction.

At the time No 58148 was one of only three of the Class still running in normal service, all allocated to Coalville. They were retained to work the branch because they could pass through the narrow Glenfield tunnel. *K. C. H. Fairey*

Right Banbury shed - a brick-built four-road structure - was completed around late August 1908. During the Second World War an enormous increase in traffic resulted in Banbury becoming an extremely important and busy railway centre. Improvements to the shed were necessary and in 1943 a lifting shop was built, provided with a 68-foot pit and 50-ton engine hoist.

Taken almost exactly 50 years after the shed's opening, this photograph shows locomotives in the sidings between the shed and the lifting shop. Adjacent to the shed stands 'Castle' Class 4-6-0 No 7032 *Denbigh Castle* (81A). In the next siding are '94XX' Class 0-6-0PT No 8452, '57XX' Class 0-6-0PT No 3646 and '5600' Class 0-6-2T No 6627. Both the pannier tanks have been coaled, but the excess on the roofs has not been removed. This was not particularly good shed practice. *D. J. Hucknall*

Left Old Oak Common 'Castle' No 7020 *Gloucester Castle* stands in a siding facing the repair shop at Oxford shed (81F). The raised roof section was to accommodate the shear legs which were used to lift a locomotive to remove the wheels. The usual paraphernalia associated with railway sheds in the days of steam - a discarded shovel, an abandoned wheelbarrow - can clearly be seen.

In the late 1950s Oxford shed had an allocation of 64 locomotives, including four 'Castles' of its own (Nos 5012/25/33 and 7008) that worked to Chester and Paddington. Oxford was a fascinating shed because main-line engines from the four regions of British Railways could regularly be seen there. It eventually closed in 1967, having served the needs of the railway system for well over one hundred years. *D. J Hucknall Collection*

Above Inside its home shed on 12 August 1957, Penzance's 'Grange' No 6870 *Bodicote Grange* (83G, February 1957-January 1960) is being prepared for duty. The engineman obviously cares enough about his work and the locomotive to clean its top sides. From Penzance No 6870 moved to Truro, where it stayed until September 1961. My lasting memory of this scene will always be of the huge volume of unpleasant green-yellow smoke that billowed from the chimney and, at times, spread beyond the confines of the smoke duct. *D. J. Hucknall*

Left With their fires completely dropped, 'Grange' No 6800 *Arlington Grange* and a couple of 'Halls' stand on one of the four roads inside Penzance shed. While an engine was cold, repairs that could not otherwise be considered were carried out. From the pools of water and the abandoned hose, it seems that one engine at least has had a boiler washout.

The smell of a locomotive shed is hard to describe. Walking between the engines, waves of smells are encountered - here paraffin, there lubricating oil, next saturated steam - all contributing to the indescribable atmosphere. *D. J. Hucknall*

8. Ready to go

Over the years, such respected authors as O. S. Nock and C. J. Allen travelled the length and breadth of the country timing trains, and many engine crews acquired well-deserved reputations for distinguished work on Britain's top expresses as a result of their articles and books. The East Coast Main Line had, for example, drivers such as Hoole and Hailstone at King's Cross and Swan and Nairn at Haymarket. The Southern Region had Tutt and Gingell at Stewarts Lane.

Although receiving much less publicity, drivers such as Carruthers and Stalker (Carlisle Upperby), Newcombe and Hammett (Laira) and Edwards (Kentish Town), and many, many others, were responsible for outstanding runs on their allotted routes. It is the way of the world, however, that their partners, the firemen - often shifting tons of coal on a long, fast run - received much less attention.

While a locomotive was running the duties of the crew were fairly clear cut. It was the driver's responsibility to run his train safely, economically and to schedule, while the fireman was concerned with the efficient generation of steam. Both before and after the journey, however, the engine was in the hands of firedroppers, cleaners, boilersmiths and other essential members of the shed staff.

Steam locomotive depots employed considerable numbers of people. According to H. G. Forsythe (*Men of Steam*, Atlantic Books 1982), King's Cross shed employed 1,100. Of the 1,000 at Old Oak Common, approximately 800 were drivers and firemen. Career progression in the old days of steam was extremely slow. In the inter-war period it could have taken 30 years to work through the ranks from cleaner to driver and onwards. It was supposed to introduce a man to his profession.

At the beginning of his work the driver of an engine would collect from the shed stores cylinder oil and lubricating oil. The fireman would obtain a shovel, coal hammer and various tools, lamps and other necessary equipment. Generally the engine was partially prepared before the crew arrived. The fire would be relatively small, and the first task of the fireman was to built it up by spreading it over the grate and adding fairly large lumps of coal. It was not unusual to add almost a ton before departure from the shed. The smoke produced by a recently lit fire did not have the pleasant smell of that from a hot locomotive. It had a choking, sooty quality and, because the blower could not be used, it evolved slowly from the chimney to be wafted by any vague wind.

While the fire was burning through, the fireman would tighten the smokebox door, check the cleanliness of the ashpan and satisfy himself that injectors, gauges and the blower were working. The driver would be examining the locomotive in great detail, topping up mechanical lubricators and oiling vital components.

D. J. Fleming, who had been closely associated with St Philips Marsh shed, remembers early Monday mornings '. . . when you could not see across the shed with all the numerous engines being prepared for their duties. . . I remembered the atmosphere of it all; flare lamps glowing in the dark; flickering shadows; the sound of blowers operating, the singing of safety valves . . . the thud of coal picks, the ringing of shovels. . .'

When new, Peppercorn 4-6-2 No 60530 *Sayajirao* was stationed at King's Cross mpd, moving to New England shed in December 1948. On 9 January 1950 she went to Haymarket shed in Edinburgh, staying there for over ten years. Late in her career, the transfers were frequent - St Margarets (16 October 1961), Polmadie (15 September 1963), Dundee (31 July 1964). In this photograph No 60530 is shown being serviced at St Margarets. In the background a DMU rushes past on the main line. *D. J. Hucknall*

Above V2' Class 2-6-2 No 60824 stands quietly at St Margarets on 20 June 1965. Over the years, 64A had a number of 'V2s' in its allocation, No 60824 arriving in November 1959 from Ferryhill via Haymarket mpd. With their high power ('6MT') and short wheelbase, the 'V2s' were ideally suited to the difficult Waverley route between Carlisle and Edinburgh. One can imagine them on their way to Edinburgh, initially blasting their way up the 3½ miles at 1 in 100 to Penton and, later, up the 1 in 70 for 9½ miles to Whitrope summit. There was yet another climb, for 15½ miles up the valley of Gala Water from Galashiels to Falahill box, at an average gradient of 1 in 150, before the descent to Edinburgh began. *D. J. Hucknall*

Below Standard Class '5' 4-6-0 No 73106 (63A) looks quite magnificent as she stands at Eastfield shed, Glasgow, on 9 June 1960. Fresh from Cowlairs Works, she would have been running in and the crew appear to be concerned with the right-hand injector exhaust. Also in the picture, on the right, one of Hurlford's Standard Class '3' 2-6-0s, No 77019, appears to have recently emerged from the Works. *W. A. C. Smith*

In connection with the Scottish Industries Exhibition that was held at Kelvin Hall, Glasgow, a programme of special excursions was organised during the first fortnight in September 1959. Four preserved pre-1923 locomotives (*City of Truro, Gordon Highlander, No 123, and Glen Douglas*) were involved. On 5 September *City of Truro* and *Gordon Highlander* had hauled one of the specials from Aberdeen to Glasgow, and are shown here being prepared for the 7.30 pm return at Polmadie shed under the gaze of a crew member. *W. A. C. Smith*

Waiting at Polmadie shed on 24 June 1960 to work overnight Anglo-Scottish trains are Bank Hall's 'Jubilee' No 45717 *Dauntless*, Camden's 'Coronation' No 46246 *City of Manchester* and Polmadie's 'Coronation' No 46224 *Princess Alexandra*. In the 1950s there were five sleeping-car departures from Glasgow Central between 9.25 and 11.30 pm - three to London, one to Birmingham and a combined Liverpool/Manchester. The Stanier 'Pacifics' were responsible for most of the London and Birmingham workings while 'Royal Scots', 'Jubilees' and 'Clans' (later 66A 'Britannias') were in charge of the Lancashire trains. The 66A '8P' on the Glasgow-Birmingham trains was changed either at Carlisle or Crewe. *W. A. C. Smith*

Above Men and locomotives going about their work at Polmadie on 12 August 1958. With its cylinder cocks open and escaping steam stabbing the air, a 2-6-4T coupled behind rebuilt 'Patriot' Class No 45528 (then un-named) leaves 66A for its next duty, whilst a footplateman strides purposefully towards the shed. No 45528 was on its way to Glasgow Central station to pick up the 5.40 pm to Euston in place of 'Princess Royal' Class No 46203 *Princess Margaret Rose* which had become derailed on the ashpits. The 5.40 pm must have put its passengers through quite an ordeal - it took a staggering 11¼ hours to complete its journey. *W. A. C. Smith*

Below Outside Helensburgh shed on a cold February day in 1960 stands begrimed 'V3' Class 2-6-2T No 67628. The depot had about 14 engines in

mid-November 1959, including ten of the 'V1/V3' Class (Nos 67604/13/14/16/19/22/25/28/31/32). They worked the 24 daily passenger trains, mainly to Bridgeton Cross but also to Dumbarton and to Singer (where there was, of course, a sewing machine factory).

On Friday 4 November 1960 the last regular steam-hauled train (it was thought) between Glasgow and Helensburgh Central left Queen Street Low Level station. The following day the first stage of the 25kV ac Glasgow Suburban Electrification was officially opened. Initial problems, however, led to the rapid substitution of steam services for a while, but, in reality, the work of the 2-6-2Ts was over. In December 1962 No 67628 was transferred to Gateshead. There it worked with others of the Class on parcels and empty stock trains. It was withdrawn two years later. *W. A. C. Smith*

Left The essence of the engine shed has been captured, as it has in most of his photographs in this book, by Bill Smith. Taken on 15 April 1963 it shows 'Clan' 4-6-2 No 72006 *Clan McKenzie*, Ivatt 2-6-0 No 46467 and Stanier 'Black Five' No 44795 outside Stranraer shed. From the beginning of the Second World War until 1952 the Glasgow-Stranraer line was worked by 'Jubilees' and 'Black Fives'.

In 1952, however, the BR 'Clans' began work on an intensive turn from Carlisle involving the 3.16 am Carlisle-Stranraer Harbour parcels, the 11.44 am Stranraer-Glasgow, 5.10 pm Glasgow-Stranraer and the 12.10 am Stranraer Harbour-Carlisle parcels. The poor old 'Clans' were indifferent performers. According to Derek Cross, writing in *The Railway Magazine* in July 1952, with trains heavier than three to five vehicles they steamed badly and slipped significantly, particularly on the climb from Creetown to Gatehouse of Fleet. *W. A. C. Smith*

Below Beattock bank is the name given to the 12-mile-long climb, mostly at 1 in 75, through the 'silent miles of wind-bent grasses' between the Lowther Hills and the heights of Tweedsmuir on the Carlisle-Glasgow main line. Such was the severity of the climb on the south side that, in the days of the steam locomotive, many northbound trains would have to opt for banking assistance at Beattock station prior to the gruelling climb ahead.

Over the years ex-Caledonian Railway 4-6-2Ts and 0-4-4Ts were used as bankers, but, towards the end, Fairburn Class '4MTs' were the preferred type. Here, on 4 August 1962, bankers Nos 42214 and 42239 stand outside the shed. On my only visit to Beattock in March 1965, Nos 42060, 42214, 42688 and 42693 were 'on shed'. The shed survived until the end of steam on the Scottish Region, but in May 1967 it closed and its last two locomotives went for scrap. *W. A. C. Smith*

Britannia' 'Pacific' No 70053 *Moray Firth* was completed (together with No 70052) at Crewe Works around late August 1954, and the pair were sent to Polmadie to join Nos 70050/51. Initially they joined the 'Clans' on workings between Glasgow and Liverpool such as the 7.24 pm arrival at Liverpool (Exchange) from Glasgow and the 9.43 am return. Within a couple of months, however, they had virtually ousted the 'Clans'.

In October 1958 No 70053 was transferred to Holbeck where it was used to work trains such as the 'Thames-Clyde Express'. It was transferred to the Midland Region in August 1962, and by October 1965 the former Polmadie 'Britannias' were found working from Banbury together with a motley collection of locomotives including '8Fs' and 'Black Fives'.

When this photograph was taken on 2 January 1966, Banbury had a further nine months before closure, whereafter *Moray Firth* and her sisters returned to the north once more, this time to Kingmoor. *D. J. Hucknall*

Above On the afternoon of 6 August 1958 '9F' Class 2-10-0 No 92226 slowly draws away from Banbury shed, cylinder cocks open and fierce jets of steam piercing the air. The '9Fs' were allocated to Banbury to replace some Stanier '8F' 2-8-0s that had been transferred there in 1955.

Ironstone, originating either in Northamptonshire or in the wolds on the Leicestershire/Nottinghamshire borders, was an important commodity required by the steel industry of South Wales. Motive power for the ironstone trains between Banbury and South Wales was provided by the '9Fs' that worked to Cardiff, Llanwern and Severn Tunnel Junction. Banbury's '9Fs' were not used exclusively on these trains and were also to be found on trains to Birkenhead and Reading. *D. J. Hucknall*

Left A branch-line tank engine - 'O2' Class 0-4-4T No 30193, a design introduced by Adams for the LSWR in 1889 - stands outside Friary shed, Plymouth, on 25 August 1959. Friary's work included local passenger duties, and the 'O2s' were used on branch-line services such as that between there and Turnchapel and locals to St Budeaux, Gunnislake and Tavistock. The 'O2s' only weighed about 47 tons and the heavier (60 tons 4 cwt) and more powerful 'M7s' eventually arrived to work services such as the Tavistock-Okehampton and Brent locals. *K. C. H. Fairey*

9. Duties

The function of the shed and its personnel was to provide men and locomotives to carry out the allotted tasks. Enginemen at a shed were divided into 'links', and the duties covered by each link were well defined. A medium-sized shed such as Banbury would have links to deal with the vacuum-piped goods trains, excursions, crew relief for goods trains passing through the area, branch-line trains, etc. A large shed such as St Margarets would have to deal with fast freights on the East Coast Main Line or the Waverley route, dock shunting, routine work in colliery sidings, empty stock, and so on. Depending on the shed, its duties, its allocated engines and even the weather, footplate work could be exhilarating and fulfilling, or grim and arduous, delightfully easy or stultifyingly boring.

Record-breaking performances on express trains have been chronicled extensively over the years by authors such as P. Ransome Wallis and O. S. Nock, but often the most telling accounts of locomotive work come from the enginemen themselves. Harold Gasson (in *Nostalgic Days*, OPC 1980) describes so well the satisfaction of a job well done. After a long hard struggle with a poor engine and a heavy freight, the end of the duty was in sight. He recalls:

'As the sinking sun caught us, that old locomotive became a thing of beauty . . . the shadows of the engine ran with us in soft outline, sliding over the meadows and cornfields, slipping over hedges and ditches . . . the feather of steam from the safety valve, a wisp of steam escaping from the whistle. . .'

A highly readable account of a footplate trip from Water Orton, Birmingham, to Carlisle with a freight train hauled by '9F' No 92165 is given by P. Ransome Wallis (*Trains Illustrated*, November 1959).

'From Settle Junction,' he recounts, 'this was one of the most memorable trips ever made on an engine in Britain. With the regulator fully open and the cut-off brought back by stages from 15 to 40 per cent, No 92165 roared up the long bank . . . throwing smoke and coal dust in clouds from the chimney but with a perfect beat. . . A crisp, clear, moonlit night added beauty and exhilaration to our progress, and the shadow of the engine was often clearly defined on the moorland hills.'

Dusty, dirty Class '2F' 0-6-0 No 57326 acts as pilot on Motherwell shed on 2 March 1963. In a large depot such as this, the loco shunt was a very necessary duty, involving replacing filled wagons on the ashpit with empties and assembling wagons for the coaling plant.

The '2F' 'Jumbos' were introduced in 1883 as the standard goods design of Dugald Drummond. In total 244 locomotives were produced (by Drummond and his successors) in the period to 1897. As late as 1959, nearly half the stock was still in existence.

The winter of 1962/63 was awful and several other Caley veterans were in steam on that day in March. They had been returned to service because of the unreliability of the Clayton diesels in the freezing weather. *W. A. C. Smith*

Above 'And what a joy it has been to travel behind a "Duchess" storming up Shap on a moonlit night . . . that crisp, deep and beautifully even exhaust echoing across the fells.' This sentence, taken from an article by D. F. Tee in the *Railway Observer* of November 1964 expresses perfectly the feelings of many years towards these superb locomotives. Workings such as the 'Mid-day Scot' demanded carefully prepared engines in first-rate condition. In this photograph of 'Coronation' Class No 46249 *City of Sheffield* at Glasgow Central on 22 April 1954, this aspect of shed work is brilliantly exemplified. The tender, coaled with fuel of exceptional uniformity and trimmed to perfection, and the locomotive, with the safety valves lightly lifting, speak volumes for the care and competence of the shed staff at Polmadie. *W. A. C. Smith*

Below A further example of the work of a dedicated preparation team - absolutely beautiful 'Castle' No 7029 *Clun Castle* stands at Newcastle Central station in September 1967 on one of her

forays to the north that year. She has been burnished to near perfection, and her smokebox, copper-capped chimney, even the buffers, have received minute attention. It was not too many years before Newcastle would also have been graced by Haymarket and King's Cross 'Pacifics' similarly sparkling as they worked the 'Elizabethan'.

No 7029 moved from Newton Abbot to Old Oak Common in August 1962. While there she was chosen to haul the return leg of a special from Paddington to Plymouth to mark the 60th anniversary of the record run of the 'Ocean Mail' on 9 May 1904. The comments of a passenger in the second coach from the engine on No 7029's climb to Whiteball were reported by O. S. Nock (*The Railway Magazine*, October 1964): 'The roar from the chimney was so colossal that even shouted conversation was almost impossible. The individual beats had merged into one continuous roar.' *D. J. Hucknall*

Above Acting as shed pilot on 12 April 1964, '8F' Class 2-8-0 No 48665 backs on to empties on the road leading up to the coal stage at Canklow mpd. Clearly visible in this photograph, above the forward and centre driving wheels, are the tops to the sandbox fillers. The sandboxes were filled via a cranked tube, some six inches in diameter. It was very hard work lugging filled sand buckets up to the running plate and it was usual to assume that if sand could be seen at the tube bottom, then the boxes were full enough. *D. J. Hucknall*

Left Rapid progress is necessary for Robinson Class 'O4/1' 2-8-0 No 63736 (built August 1912; withdrawn August 1963) as she is occupying the up East Coast Main Line near Ranskill on the evening of 14 June 1957. The fact that the first four vans of this freight train were from the SNCF was unusual. Tender-first running was uncomfortable for the crew because of coal dust blowing from the tender. *D. J. Hucknall*

Right Looking for the 'right away' from King's Cross station, a crew member leans well out of the cab of 'A1' No 60156 *Great Central*. This Class was one of the most consistent and reliable ever to run on Britain's railways. No 60156 was one of six 'A1s' allocated to Grantham shed's top link in the mid-1950s when that depot was responsible for many East Coast Main Line expresses, including the down 'Flying Scotsman', 'Aberdonian', and up 'Heart of Midlothian'. In September 1956, when through workings between Newcastle and King's Cross were reintroduced, Grantham's 'A1s' were sent to King's Cross shed. In the few years it spent there, No 60156 was possibly the shed's most dependable locomotive. One of her regular drivers was Horace Duckmanton whose outstanding work over the years was admirably highlighted by P. J. Coster (see *SLS Journal*, August/September 1968) and complemented by this remarkable locomotive. *D. J. Hucknall Collection*

Above left The crew of '2251' Class No 2259 pass a quiet spell in the sidings near Banbury shed on an afternoon in August 1957. Seeing the photographer, one of the enginemen raises a mug of tea in salute.

The '2251s', designed by Collett and introduced in 1930, were ideal for the work they carried out (mainly hard branch-line working). Boiler pressure was 200 lbs and the cylinders were 17½ inches in diameter with a 24-inch stroke. They had power without too much weight. From this photograph No 2259 appears to be fitted with an ex-ROD tender which, at 47 tons 6 cwt, would have weighed more than the locomotive (43 tons 10 cwt). *D. J. Hucknall*

Left One of Collett's '1400' Class 0-4-2 ('1P') tank engines, No 1474, stands at Berkeley Road on 4 April 1964, having worked the auto-train to and from Lydney. Introduced in 1932, the Class was designed for light branch work, and I found them immensely appealing - together with the

'4500s' they remain a constant reminder of the beauty of many of the English branch lines. Colin Gifford's photograph of No 1473 dashing down to Saunderton, with its driver seated and smiling (see *Decline of Steam* by C. T. Gifford) is, in my opinion, an unbeatable record of the Class in service. *D. J. Hucknall*

Above Britain's railwaymen worked their way slowly through the hierarchy from engine cleaning to firing to driving. It was a process that took many years and involved arduous and sometimes dangerous work at unsociable hours. They were men who were respected in their communities and who contributed immeasurably to the wealth of the country.

In this undated photograph, the photographer has captured superbly two unknown railwaymen. Doubtless, and justifiably, proud of their gleaming 'Hall', No 7908 *Henshall Hall* (Tyseley), they await the 'right away' from Reading. *H. G. Usmar*

With a background of Bristol Bath Road shed, final preparations are made to 'Castle' Class 4-6-0 No 5003 *Lulworth Castle* prior to departure from Temple Meads station. A complement of trainspotters has converged on the engine and one of them is about to 'footplate' the 'Castle'. The fireman is attending to his fire with a dart. Part of the art of the fireman was to deal with the clinker that blocked the airspaces in the grate and prevented air admitted through the dampers from reaching the fire. With the dart he would break up and dislodge any clinker, and a pricker would be used to clear out airspaces in the grate. The best safeguard was to spread a bucketful of firebrick or limestone over the grate before the fire was built up. *H. G. Usmar*

Above Unrebuilt 'West Country' Class 4-6-2 No 34105 *Swanage* moves 'off shed' at Ropley on the Mid-Hants Railway on 24 April 1988. Ropley was on the single-line Alton-Winchester branch, but in fact never had a railway shed. Indeed, the locomotive headcode would, in earlier days, have indicated a train running between Waterloo or Nine Elms and Southampton Terminus via Alton.

The line came into its own during disruptions to the main line further east when it would be used by Bournemouth line trains, diverted via Farnborough. On 23 August 1955, for example, engineering work at Farnborough caused diversion of the 9.20 am, 9.35 am and 10.14 am from Waterloo via Alton. They were hauled by Nos 34018 *Axminster*, 30858 *Lord Duncan* and 35019 *French Line* CGT respectively. Pilot locomotives were often used on the steep gradients between Alton and Alresford. *D. J. Hucknall*

Right A picture that truly does justice to the beautifully proportioned rebuilt Bulleid 'Pacifics'. 'West Country' Class No 34016 *Bodmin* has left the shed at Ropley and is preparing to reverse down to Alresford station to begin the day's work. Clearly visible on the bright spring morning are the large-diameter cast iron chimney and, on the footplating along the side of the engine, two of the engine's lubricators. The rebuilds had three six-feed Wakefield mechanical lubricators for the cylinders and steamchests and a ten-feed lubricator (visible here with one of the Wakefield six-feeds) supplying engine oil to the coupled axles. *D. J. Hucknall*

10. The end

In the face of increasing dieselisation and electrification, the decline of steam and, with it, that of the steam motive power depot was inexorable. Examples from a list of sheds closed to steam at the time made depressing reading: Cricklewood (14.12.64); Reading (4.1.65); Bushbury (12.4.65); Crewe North (14.6.65); Dalry Road (3.10.65); Banbury (3.10.66); Tyseley (7.11.66), and so on.

Some closures had significance far beyond the importance of the shed. For example, when Nuneaton's depot closed in June 1966 there were no steam depots south of Crewe on the London Midland main line via the Trent Valley. When Tyseley was closed in November 1966, steam on the Western Region's West Midlands lines was largely confined to the Wolverhampton area (Oxley shed continued with steam operations). In sharp contrast, the scrapyards became increasingly crowded (at Barry Docks at the end of July 1966 there were 172 locomotives including six 'Merchant Navies' and eight 'Manors').

I left Scotland in late 1965, and by the end of 1966 the elimination of steam was very advanced. Few trains were steam-hauled and even then they were restricted to perhaps three operations, including coal traffic from Fife and various freight/parcels workings to and from Carlisle. My shed visits became fewer and fewer as the condition of locomotives deteriorated, and I feel that my last sight of a British Railways steam locomotive in revenue-earning service was of an 'Austerity' (almost inevitably) pulling empty mineral wagons through Gateshead.

Today almost all the railway sheds that were once so important to the economic life of Britain have gone forever. True, there are here and there examples of intact working sheds (usually, as in the cases of Didcot and Carnforth, associated with preservation societies), but it is easy to assume that bulldozers and tarmac have removed forever any trace of their existence. If, however, we are prepared to look carefully, in the weeds and shrubs, near some old track, the outline of the shed building or the coaling stage or the turntable pit may yet be found.

On the morning of 2 March 1965 the former Gateshead 'A4' No 60016 *Silver King* stands in store at the rear of Perth shed. Having been transferred to St Margarets on 28 October 1963, within two weeks she was moved to Ferryhill. Condemned some 17 days after this photograph was taken, she was scrapped in May 1965.

Perth mpd was a typical 1930s LMS structure, made of brick, steel and corrugated sheet. It had replaced two Perth sheds (North and South) that had been used to house Highland Railway and Caledonian Railway engines respectively. *D. J. Hucknall*

Above The evening sun on 3 June 1963 dapples the boiler of 'A1' Class 4-6-2 No 60154 *Bon Accord*, also in store at York South shed. *Bon Accord* was one of five 'A1s' (Nos 60153-7) fitted with roller bearings. During their working lives, the five were wonderfully reliable, Nos 60154 and 60155 *Borderer* being outstanding. On her withdrawal No 60154 had covered 1,035,000 miles.

On the right stands stored 'V2' No 60831. Transferred to 50A in September 1959 from the former Great Central depot at Woodford Halse, she survived until December 1966, to be scrapped in the following February by Drapers in Hull. *D. J. Hucknall*

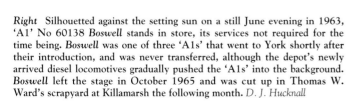

Right Silhouetted against the setting sun on a still June evening in 1963, 'A1' No 60138 *Boswell* stands in store, its services not required for the time being. *Boswell* was one of three 'A1s' that went to York shortly after their introduction, and was never transferred, although the depot's newly arrived diesel locomotives gradually pushed the 'A1s' into the background. *Boswell* left the stage in October 1965 and was cut up in Thomas W. Ward's scrapyard at Killamarsh the following month. *D. J. Hucknall*

Above Without prospect of work, covered with grime and denied even their nameplates, a line of four 'Jubilees' stands at Carlisle Kingmoor in March 1965; shown here are Nos 45629 *Straits Settlements*, 45742 *Connaught* and 45574 *India*.

Connaught, a Bushbury engine for many years, was fitted with a double chimney from mid-1940 until November 1955 and was a very economical, freely steaming engine, figuring prominently on the 2-hour Wolverhampton/Birmingham-Euston trains. At the start of the 1959 winter timetables, all Bushbury's 'Jubilees', including No 45742, were transferred to Carlisle Upperby. *India*, among other things, was notable for having hauled the last LMS train to arrive at Euston on 31 December 1947; she drew in at 11.55 pm, and at midnight British Railways came into existence. *Connaught* was withdrawn in May 1965; *India* survived for another year. *D. J. Hucknall*

Left Collett's '14XX' and '58XX' Class 0-4-2T locomotives were built for branch-line work, for which job they were perfect - the boiler pressure was only 165 lbs, 800 gallons of water were carried and the weight was just over 40 tons. They will always be associated in my mind with rural English branch lines in the *Titfield Thunderbolt* tradition.

Even withdrawn and in a dilapidated state, No 5815 is still a proud and pleasing engine with her tall chimney and large driving wheels. Looking at her, one remembers a verse from 'Dilton Marsh Halt' by John Betjeman:

'And when all the horrible roads are finally done for,
And there's no more petrol left in the world to burn,
Here to the Halt from Salisbury and from Bristol
Steam trains will return.'

D. J. Hucknall Collection

The end at Okehampton - gone are the steam locomotives, gone is the shed. The only things remaining by July 1965 are the water column and, of course, a wagon of ash. *D. J. Hucknall*

The railway from Gwinear Road to Helston opened on 9 May 1887, and closed to passengers on 3 November 1962 and to goods traffic on 4 October 1964. By the end of July 1965, after almost 80 years of railway operation, only a derelict signal, broken and rusting, remains at Helston; the taller arm had been the up main starter and the shorter the up main to loco starter. In the background, behind the base of the signal, can be seen what remained of the shed and the wall of the ash hopper. *D. J. Hucknall*

Its services long dispensed with and now marked by passing birds, '45XX' Class 2-6-2T No 5537 stands in Penzance shed yard at Long Rock in August 1963. For a long time she had been stationed at Truro, working the branch line to Falmouth with her sisters. It was the increasing use of diesel multiple units in Devon and Cornwall during the summer of 1961 that accelerated the withdrawal of the 'Prairie' tanks. No 5537 moved to Penzance in January 1962 and was withdrawn from that shed in the following August. *D. J. Hucknall*

Appendix 1
British Railways locomotive sheds and shed codes, 1956/7

London Midland Region

1A Willesden
1B Camden
1C Watford
1D Devons Road (Bow)
1E Bletchley
    Leighton Buzzard

2A Rugby
    Seaton
2B Nuneaton
2C Warwick
2D Coventry
2E Northampton
2F Market Harborough

3A Bescot
3B Bushbury
3C Walsall
3D Aston
3E Monument Lane

5A Crewe North
    Whitchurch
5B Crewe South
5C Stafford
5D Stoke
5E Alsager
5F Uttoxeter

6A Chester
6B Mold Junction
6C Birkenhead
6D Chester (Northgate)
6E Wrexham
6F Bidston
6G Llandudno Junction
6H Bangor
6J Holyhead
6K Rhyl

8A Edge Hill
8B Warrington
    Warrington
    (Arpley)
8C Speke Junction
8D Widnes
8E Brunswick
    (Liverpool)

9A Longsight
9B Stockport (Edgeley)
9C Macclesfield
9D Buxton
9E Trafford Park
9F Heaton Mersey
9G Northwich

10A Springs Branch
    (Wigan)
10B Preston
10C Patricroft
10D Sutton Oak

11A Carnforth
11B Barrow
    Coniston
11C Oxenholme
11D Tebay
11E Lancaster

12A Carlisle (Upperby)
12B Penrith
12C Workington

14A Cricklewood
14B Kentish Town
14C St Albans

15A Wellingborough
15B Kettering
15C Leicester
15D Bedford

16A Nottingham
16B Kirkby
16C Mansfield

17A Derby
17B Burton
    Horninglow
    Overseal
17C Coalville
17D Rowsley
    Cromford
    Middleton
    Sheep Pasture

18A Toton
18B Westhouses
18C Hasland
18D Staveley
    Sheepbridge

19A Sheffield
19B Millhouses
19C Canklow

20A* Leeds (Holbeck)
    Keighley
20B* Stourton
20C* Royston
20D* Normanton
20E* Manningham
    Ilkley
20F Skipton
20G Hellifield

21A Saltley
21B Bournville
21C Bromsgrove

22A Bristol
22B Gloucester
    Dursley
    Tewkesbury

24A Accrington
24B Rose Grove

24C Lostock Hall
24D Lower Darwen
24E Blackpool
    Blackpool North
24F Fleetwood

25A* Wakefield
25B* Huddersfield
25C* Goole
25D* Mirfield
25E* Sowerby Bridge
25F* Low Moor
25G* Farnley Junction

26A Newton Heath
26B Agecroft
26C Bolton
26D Bury
26E Lees

27A Bank Hall
27B Aintree
27C Southport
27D Wigan (L&Y)
27E Walton

Eastern Region

30A Stratford
    Brentwood
    Chelmsford
    Enfield Town
    Epping
    Ilford
    Wood St
    (Walthamstow)
30B Hertford East
    Buntingford
    Ware
30C Bishops Stortford
30D Southend (Victoria)
    Southminster
30E Colchester
    Braintree
    Clacton
    Maldon
    Walton-on-Naze
30F Parkeston

31A Cambridge
    Ely
    Huntingdon East
    Saffron Walden
31B March
    Wisbech
31C King's Lynn
    Hunstanton
31D South Lynn
31E Bury St Edmunds
    Sudbury (Suffolk)

32A Norwich
    Cromer Beach
    Swaffham
    Wymondham
32B Ipswich
    Aldeburgh
    Felixstowe Beach
    Stowmarket
32C Lowestoft
32D Yarmouth (South
    Town)
32E Yarmouth
    (Vauxhall)
32F Yarmouth Beach
32G Melton Constable
    Norwich City

33A Plaistow
    Upminster
33B Tilbury
33C Shoeburyness

34A King's Cross
34B Hornsey
34C Hatfield
34D Hitchin
34E Neasden
    Aylesbury
    Chesham

35A New England
    Spalding
    Stamford
35B Grantham
35C Peterborough
    (Spital)

36A Doncaster
36B Mexborough
    Wath
36C Frodingham
36D Barnsley
36E Retford
    Newark

38A Colwick
38B Annesley
38C Leicester (GC)
38D Staveley
38E Woodford Halse

39A Gorton
    Dinting
    Hayfield

40A Lincoln
    Lincoln (St Marks)
40B Immingham
    Grimsby
    New Holland
40C Louth
40D Tuxford
40E Langwith Junction
40F Boston

*See NE Region Codes 53,
55 and 56*

41A Sheffield (Darnall)

North Eastern Region

50A York
50B Leeds (Neville Hill)
50C Selby
50D Starbeck
50E Scarborough
50F Malton
    Pickering
50G Whitby

51A Darlington
    Middleton-in-
    Teesdale
51B Newport (Yorks)
51C West Hartlepool
51D Middlesbrough
51E Stockton
51F West Auckland
51G Haverton Hill
51H Kirkby Stephen
51J Northallerton
51K Saltburn

52A Gateshead
    Bowes Bridge
52B Heaton
52C Blaydon
    Alston
    Hexham
52D Tweedmouth
    Alnmouth
52E Percy Main
52F North Blyth
    South Blyth

53A Hull (Dairycoates)
53B Hull (Botanic
    Gardens)
53C Hull (Springhead)
    Alexandra Dock
53D Bridlington
53E* Goole (25C)

54A Sunderland
    Durham
54B Tyne Dock
54C Borough Gardens
54D Consett

55A* Leeds (Holbeck)
    (20A)
55B* Stourton (20B)
55C* Farnley Junction
    (25G)
55D* Royston (20C)
55E* Normanton (20D)
55F* Manningham (20E)
    Ilkley
55G* Huddersfield (25B)

56A* Wakefield (25A)
56B Ardsley

56C	Copley Hill		Dunbar		Winchester	82B	St Philip's Marsh	86A	Newport (Ebbw
56D*	Mirfield (25D)		Galashiels	71B	Bournemouth	82C	Swindon		Junction)
56E*	Sowerby Bridge		Longniddry		Branksome		Chippenham	86B	Newport (Pill)
	(25E)		North Berwick	71G	Bath (S&D)	82D	Westbury	86C	Cardiff (Canton)
56F*	Low Moor (25F)	64B	Haymarket		Radstock		Frome	86D	Llantrisant
56G	Bradford	64C	Dalry Road	71H	Templecombe	82E	Yeovil	86E	Severn Tunnel
		64D	Carstairs	71I	Southampton Docks	82F	Weymouth		Junction
Scottish Region		64E	Polmont	71J	Highbridge		Bridport	86F	Tondu
		64F	Bathgate					86G	Pontypool Road
60A	Inverness	64G	Hawick	72A	Exmouth Junction	83A	Newton Abbot		Abergavenny
	Dingwall		Riccarton		Bude		Ashburton	86H	Aberbeeg
	Kyle of Lochalsh		St Boswells		Exmouth		Kingsbridge	86J	Aberdare
60B	Aviemore				Lyme Regis	83B	Taunton	86K	Tredegar
	Boat of Garten	65A	Eastfield (Glasgow)		Okehampton		Bridgwater		
60C	Helmsdale	65B	St Rollox		Seaton		Minehead	87A	Neath
	Dornock	65C	Parkhead	72B	Salisbury	83C	Exeter		Glyn Neath
	Tain	65D	Dawsholm	72C	Yeovil		Tiverton Junction		Neath (N&B)
60D	Wick		Dumbarton	72D	Plymouth	83D	Laira (Plymouth)	87B	Duffryn Yard
	Thurso	65E	Kipps		Callington		Launceston	87C	Danygraig
60E	Forres	65F	Grangemouth	72E	Barnstaple Junction	83E	St Blazey	87D	Swansea East Dock
		65G	Yoker		Ilfracombe		Bodmin	87E	Landore
61A	Kittybrewster	65H	Helensburgh		Torrington		Moorswater	87F	Llanelly
	Ballater	65I	Balloch	72F	Wadebridge	83F	Truro		Burry Port
	Fraserburgh	65J	Fort William			83G	Penzance		Pantyfynnon
	Inverurie		Mallaig	73A	Stewarts Lane		Helston	87G	Carmarthen
	Peterhead			73B	Bricklayers Arms		St Ives	87H	Neyland
61B	Aberdeen (Ferryhill)	66A	Polmadie (Glasgow)	73C	Hither Green				Cardigan
61C	Keith	66B	Motherwell	73D	Gillingham (Kent)	84A	Wolverhampton		Milford Haven
	Banff	66C	Hamilton	73E	Faversham		(Stafford Road)		Pembroke Dock
	Elgin	66D	Greenock			84B	Oxley		Whitland
			(Ladyburn)	74A	Ashford (Kent)	84C	Banbury	87J	Goodwick
62A	Thornton		Greenock (Princes	74B	Ramsgate	84D	Leamington Spa	87K	Swansea (Victoria)
	Anstruther		Pier)	74C	Dover	84E	Tyseley		Gurnos
	Burntisland				Folkestone		Stratford-on-Avon		Llandovery
	Ladybank	67A	Corkerhill (Glasgow)	74D	Tonbridge	84F	Stourbridge Junction		Upper Bank
	Methil	67B	Hurlford	74E	St Leonards	84G	Shrewsbury		
62B	Dundee (Tay Bridge		Beith				Builth Road	88A	Cardiff (Cathays)
	Arbroath		Muirkirk	75A	Brighton		Clee Hill		Radyr
	Dundee West	67C	Ayr		Newhaven		Craven Arms	88B	Cardiff East Dock
	Montrose	67D	Ardrossan	75B	Redhill		Knighton	88C	Barry
	St Andrews			75C	Norwood Junction	84H	Wellington (Salop)	88D	Merthyr
62C	Dunfermline	68A	Carlisle (Kingmoor)	75D	Horsham	84J	Croes Newydd		Cae Harris
	Alloa	68B	Dumfries	75E	Three Bridge		Bala		Dowlais Central
		68C	Stranraer	75F	Tunbridge Wells		Penmaenpool		Rhymney
63A	Perth South		Newton Stewart		West		Trawsfynydd	88E	Abercynon
	Aberfeldy	68D	Beattock			84K	Chester	88F	Treherbert
	Crieff	68E	Carlisle Canal	**Western Region**					Ferndale
63B	Stirling South					85A	Worcester		
	Killin	**Southern Region**		81A	Old Oak Common		Evesham	89A	Oswestry
	Stirling (Shore			81B	Slough		Kingham		Llanidoes
	Road)	70A	Nine Elms		Watlington	85B	Gloucester		Moat Lane
63C	Forfar	70B	Feltham	81C	Southall		Brimscombe		Welshpool (W&L)
63D	Oban	70C	Guildford	81D	Reading		Cheltenham	89B	Brecon
	Ballachulish	70D	Basingstoke		Henley-on-Thames		Cirencester		Builth Wells
		70E	Reading	81E	Didcot		Lydney	89C	Machynlleth
64A	St Margarets	70F	Fratton	81F	Oxford		Tetbury		Aberayron
	(Edinburgh)	70G	Newport (IOW)		Fairford	85C	Hereford		Aberystwyth
		70H	Ryde (IOW)				Ledbury		Aberystwyth
Altered shed codes in course				82A	Bristol (Bath Road)		Leominster		(V of R)
of adoption, former code in		71A	Eastleigh		Bath		Ross		Portmadoc
brackets.			Andover Junction		Wells	85D	Kidderminster		Pwllheli
			Lymington		Weston-super-Mare				

* Altered shed codes in course of adoption, former code in brackets.

Appendix 2
Selected shed visit logs

Ihave a passion for shed visit logs. As I pore over them, I can almost see an 'A1' at St Margarets, two or three 'Coronations' at Perth; perhaps a grey, foggy day, perhaps a spring day with clouds being driven across the sky and flashes of sun transforming the rows of locomotives.

My own records are few and far between - one or two from Penzance and Banbury in the late 1950s, lists of Scottish shed visits in the 1964/5 period - not for me the carefully collected numbers in a hard-bound notebook, more the hastily torn scrap of paper as I leapt from my bicycle and rushed along a line of locomotives.

Obviously only a few of the following logs are my own. For the most part they have been compiled by Steve Turnbull of the Engine Shed Society; he compiles such records as a labour of love and they provide invaluable 'snapshots' of what was once an essential part of the life of this country. In choosing the logs I have tried to find ones that are as near as possible contemporary with the photographs in this book. In some cases, however, they are included because I liked the shed and I should have loved to have been there taking the numbers.

Finally, I have also included some observations which were taken at Templecombe, Bath and Radstock, which I came across by chance. I had bought one or two books that had been part of the library of the late Dr D. Cartmel, and between the pages of one of them some meticulous notes had been left. I like to think that they were taken on some sunny afternoon after a delightful day along the line. It is a great pleasure to acknowledge the work of such chroniclers.

ABERYSTWYTH.
The shed is in the fork of the Machynlleth and Carmarthen lines. The yard is visible from both lines.

Turn left outside the station into Alexandra Road, and left into Park Avenue. A path leads from the end of this road to the shed. Walking time 5 minutes.

Note.—The narrow gauge locos are kept in a small shed at the end of the Vale of Rheidol Station, on the right hand side of Park Avenue.

Aberystwyth

17 July 1955

'2251' 0-6-0:	2200, 2216, 2260
'4300' 2-6-0:	6393
'7400' 0-60PT:	7406, 7417
'Manor' 4-6-0:	7803 *Barcote Manor*, 7817 *Garsington Manor*, 7822 *Foxcote Manor*
'Dukedog' 4-4-0:	9002, 9005, 9007, 9009, 9013, 9021

ABERDEEN (Ferryhill).
The shed is on the west side of the main line just south of the junction with the Ballater line. The yard is partially visible from the line.

Turn left out of the station yard into Guild Street. Turn left into College Street, continue into South College Street, and Wellington Road. Bear left under the railway bridge and turn right along North Esplanade. Turn right into Polmuir road, and the shed entrance is on the left hand side just past the railway over-bridge. Walking time 20 minutes.

Note.—This is a joint L.N.E. and L.M.S. shed.

Aberdeen (Ferryhill)

16 November 1963

'Black 5' 4-6-0:	44705, 44720, 45136, 45359, 45400

'A4' 4-6-2:	60011 *Empire of India*, 60012 *Commonwealth of Australia*
'V2' 2-6-2:	60898, 60970, 60973
'B1' 4-6-0:	61244 *Strang Steel*, 61347, 61400
Standard '4' 2-6-0:	76104, 76107
Standard '2' 2-6-0:	78045
'Austerity' 2-8-0:	90041, 90117, 90444, 90640, 90705

30 July 1965

'Black 5' 4-6-0:	44704, 44705, 44794, 44879
'A4' 4-6-2:	60009 *Union of South Africa*, 60024 *Kingfisher*, 60026 *Miles Beevor*, 60027 *Merlin*
'A3' 4-6-2:	60052 *Prince Palatine*
'B1' 4-6-0:	61404
Standard '5' 4-6-0:	73056, 73152
'Austerity' 2-8-0:	90596
Diesels:	D357, D359, D1851, D3546, D5125, D5306, D5314, D5324

BATH 22C.
The shed is on the north side of the line west of the station. The yard is visible from the line.

Turn right outside Bath L.M.S. Station along Midland Road. Turn right into Lower Bristol Road and right again into Bridge Road. A cinder path leads to the shed from the right hand side of this road just past the railway bridge. Walking time 10 minutes.

Bath (Dr Cartmel's observations)

7 September 1956

'West Country' 4-6-2:	34042 *Dorchester*
'2P' 4-4-0:	40568, 40601, 40634, 40696, 40698
Class '2' 2-6-2T:	41241, 41242, 41243
'3F' 0-6-0:	43218 (71H)
'4F' 0-6-0:	44096, 44417 (71H), 44523, 44561, 44589
'Black 5' 4-6-0:	44679 (5A)
'3F' 0-6-0T:	47275, 47496, 47557
'7F' 2-8-0:	53801, 53804, 53806
Standard '5' 4-6-0:	73047, 73050, 73057, 73087, 73116
Standard '4' 4-6-0:	75072, 75073

BLACKPOOL 24E.
Central Shed.
The shed is on the east side of the line south of Blackpool Central Station. The yard is visible from the line.

Turn left outside the Central Station, and left again along the Promenade. After going some distance turn left into Rigby Road. The shed entrance is on the right hand side, just past the railway over bridge. Walking time 20 minutes.

A tram labelled Squires Gate runs along the Promenade to Rigby Road.

Blackpool Central

22 March 1953

Class '4' 2-6-4T:	42438, 42637
'Crab' 2-6-0:	42729, 42869
'Black 5' 4-6-0:	44731, 44733, 44778, 44876, 44897, 44929, 44934, 44947, 44950, 45077, 45212, 45415

'Patriot' 4-6-0:	45523 *Bangor*
'Jubilee' 4-6-0:	45580 *Burma*, 45584 *North West Frontier*, 45588 *Kashmir*
Class '2' 2-6-0:	46486
'3F' 0-6-0:	52157, 52240, 52459
Standard '5' 4-6-0:	73025, 73027

26 October 1963

Class '4' 2-6-4T:	42295, 42464, 42484, 42625
'Crab' 2-6-0:	42760
'Black 5' 4-6-0:	44664, 44728, 44730, 44731, 44778, 44779, 44906, 44930, 45026, 45077, 45104, 45135, 45240, 45322, 45377, 45416, 45436, 45437
'Jubilee' 4-6-0:	45703 *Thunderer*, 45705 *Seahorse*
'B1' 4-6-0:	61334

BOURNEMOUTH.
    The shed is on the north side of the line west of Bournemouth Central Station. The yard is visible from the line.
    Leave Bournemouth Central Station by the approach road, and turn left into Holdenhurst Road. Turn first left into Wellington Road, and left into Beech Road. The shed entrance is on the left hand side just before the railway under-bridge. **Walking time 10 minutes.**

Bournemouth

1 August 1961

'M7' 0-4-4T:	30031, 30050, 30108, 30110, 30379
'S15' 4-6-0:	30509, 30511
'N15' 4-6-0:	30782 *Sir Brian*
'Schools' 4-4-0:	30905 *Tonbridge*
'West Country' 4-6-2:	34004 *Yeovil*, 34008 *Padstow*, 34040 *Crewkerne*, 34047 *Callington*, 34093 *Saunton*, 34094 *Mortehoe*, 34103 *Calstock*, 34105 *Swanage*
'Battle of Britain' 4-6-2:	34085 *501 Squadron*
'Merchant Navy' 4-6-2:	35003 *Royal Mail*, 35021 *New Zealand Line*, 35027 *Port Line*
Standard '5' 4-6-0:	73020, 73085
Standard '4' 2-6-0:	76009, 76016, 76018, 76019, 76056, 76061
Diesel:	D2274

BRISTOL. (Bath Road).
    The shed is on the east side of the line at the south end of Bristol Temple Meads Station. The yard is visible from the line.
    Go straight ahead across the yard outside the main exit from Temple Meads Station. Turn left at the bottom of the hill along Bath Road. The shed entrance is a gate on the left hand side just past the railway under bridge. **Walking time 5 minutes.**

Bristol (Bath Road)

10 August 1958

'County' 4-6-0:	1003 *County of Wilts*, 1009 *County of Carmarthen*, 1011 *County of Chester*
'1400' 0-4-2T:	1454
'5700' 0-6-0PT:	3632, 3748, 3759, 7733, 8741, 8747
'Castle' 4-6-0:	4075 *Cardiff Castle*, 4079 *Pendennis Castle*, 4086 *Builth Castle*, 5048 *Earl of Devon*, 5055 *Earl of Eldon*, 5068 *Beverston Castle*, 7007 *Great Western*, 7011 *Banbury Castle*, 7015 *Carn Brea Castle*, 7018 *Drysllwyn Castle*, 7030 *Cranbrook Castle*, 7034 *Ince Castle*, 7035 *Ogmore Castle*
'5100' 2-6-2T:	4131 (for repair), 5186, 5188
'4500' 2-6-2T:	4595, 5511, 5527, 5529, 5546, 5553, 5565, 5566, 9623, 9626, 9769
'Hall' 4-6-0:	4927 *Farnborough Hall*, 4932 *Hatherton Hall*, 4960 *Pyle Hall*, 4975 *Umberslade Hall*, 4996 *Eden Hall* (repair), 5919 *Worsley Hall*, 5945 *Leckhampton Hall*,

	5964 *Wolseley Hall*, 5977 *Beckford Hall*, 5987 *Brocket Hall*, 6957 *Norcliffe Hall*
'6100' 2-6-2T:	6107, 6137
'4300' 2-6-0:	6323, 6353
'Grange' 4-6-0:	6809 *Burghclere Grange*, 6874 *Haughton Grange*
'Modified Hall' 4-6-0:	6993 *Arthog Hall*
'9400' 0-6-0PT:	9488
Class '2' 2-6-2T:	41202
Standard '3' 2-6-2T:	82040, 82041, 82042, 82043

BRISTOL. (St. Philip's Marsh).
    The shed is on the south side of the Bristol avoiding line, just before the junction with the Taunton line. The yard is visible from the line.
    Go straight ahead across the yard outside the main exit from Temple Meads Station. Turn left at the bottom of the hill along Bath Road. Pass the entrance to Bath Road Shed, and a few yards further on turn first left into an alley. (This turning is not too conspicuous.) Go through this alley and continue over the bridge at the side of the railway. Go down the steps at the end, and continue along a short road that runs parallel to, but below the railway. There is a gate opposite the end of this road and a cinder path leads through it to the shed. **Walking time 15 minutes.**

Bristol (St Philips Marsh)

20 April 1952

'1600' 0-6-0PT:	1649
'2021' 0-6-0PT:	2135
'2251' 0-6-0:	2215, 2220, 2225, 2250, 2258, 3215,
'2301' 0-6-0:	2426, 2462, 2568, 2578
'ROD' 2-8-0:	3014, 3032, 3034, 3041
'5700' 0-6-0PT:	3604, 3614, 3623, 3632, 3643, 3676, 3731, 3748, 3765, 3773, 3795, 4607, 4619, 4626, 4688, 5784, 7718, 7719, 7728, 7729, 7749, 7779, 7780, 7783, 7790, 7793, 7795, 8703, 8713, 8714, 8725, 8730, 8741, 8747
'2800' 2-8-0:	3812, 3842
'4200' 2-8-0T:	4262
'4300' 2-6-0:	4318, 5306, 5326
'Hall' 4-6-0:	4917 *Crosswood Hall*, 4944 *Middleton Hall*, 5919 *Worsley Hall*, 5938 *Stanley Hall*, 5982 *Harrington Hall*, 6925 *Hackness Hall*, 6954 *Lotherton Hall*, 6957 *Norcliffe Hall*
'5600' 0-6-2T:	6601, 6656, 6670, 6671
'Grange' 4-6-0:	6836 *Estevarney Grange*, 6845 *Paviland Grange*, 6863 *Dolhywel Grange*, 6867 *Peterston Grange*
'7200' 2-8-2T:	7201
'9400' 0-6-0PT:	8413, 9453, 9605, 9665, 9771
'Austerity' 2-8-0:	90176, 90192, 90251, 90365

27 July 1962

'County' 4-6-0:	1005 *County of Devon*, 1011 *County of Chester*, 1024 *County of Pembroke*
'1361' 0-6-0ST:	1365
'2251' 0-6-0:	2291, 3218
'2800' 2-8-0:	2822, 3830, 3837, 3854
'5700' 0-6-0PT:	3623, 3677, 3766, 4619, 4660, 7729, 8746, 8790, 8795, 9601
'Castle' 4-6-0:	4077 *Chepstow Castle*, 5040 *Stokesay Castle*, 5089 *Westminster Abbey*, 7018 *Drysllwyn Castle*
4200 2-8-0 T:	4258, 5213
'Hall' 4-6-0:	4914 *Granmore Hall*, 4918 *Dartington Hall*, 4922 *Enville Hall*, 4933 *Himley Hall*, 4942 *Maindy Hall*, 4947 *Nanhoran Hall*, 4956 *Plowden Hall*, 4968 *Shotton Hall*, 4999 *Gopsal Hall*, 5908 *Moreton Hall*, 5914 *Ripon Hall*, 5918 *Walton Hall*, 5926 *Grotrian Hall*, 5975 *Winslow Hall*, 6914 *Langton Hall*, 6919 *Tylney Hall*
'5600' 0-6-2T:	5640, 6654
'4300' 0-6-0:	6319, 6358, 6362, 6364, 7338
'6400' 0-6-0PT:	6408

Sketch plan of Canklow shed in 1955.

'Grange' 4-6-0:	6809 *Burghclere Grange*, 6811 *Cranbourne Grange*, 6814 *Enborne Grange*, 6869 *Resolven Grange*
'Modified Hall' 4-6-0:	6982 *Melmerby Hall*, 7901 *Dodington Hall*, 7907 *Hart Hall*, 7924 *Thornycroft Hall*
Class '2' 2-6-2T:	41208, 41209
Class '2' 2-6-0:	46517
Standard '3' 2-6-2T:	82035, 82037, 82038
'9F' 2-10-0:	92248
Diesel:	D3503

CANKLOW 19C.

The shed is on the west side of the Rotherham (Masboro')-Staveley line about 2 miles south of Masboro'. The yard is visible from the line.
Go straight ahead out of Masboro' Station along Station Road. Continue along Main Street passing Rotherham L.N.E. Station on the left, and Westgate Station on the right. Turn right at the square into Westgate, and continue into Canklow Road. About 1¼ miles further on turn right along Bawtry Road. Go under the railway bridge, and turn left immediately into White Hall Lane. The shed entrance is on the left hand side 300 yards further on. Walking time 60 minutes.

Canklow

Sunday 1 July 1962

'4MT' 2-6-0:	43037
'4F' 0-6-0:	44089
'5MT' 4-6-0:	44846, 45434
'Patriot' 4-6-0:	45536 *Private W. Wood VC*
'Jubilee' 4-6-0:	45615 *Malay States*, 45658 *Keyes*
'8F' 2-8-0:	48008, 48150, 48141, 48178, 48216, 48265, 48283, 48346, 48351, 48397, 48508, 48652, 48772
'B1' 4-6-0:	61083, 61093, 61165, 61316
Standard '5' 4-6-0:	73016, 73046, 73068, 73074, 73130
Standard '4' 2-6-0:	76088
'Austerity' 2-8-0:	90276, 90391, 90414, 90471, 90719

CARDIFF (Canton).

The shed is on the south side of the main line west of Cardiff General Station. The yard is visible from the line.
Turn left outside Cardiff General Station along Saunders Road. Turn left along Wood Street, continue along Tudor Road, and then Ninian Park Road. Turn left into De Croche Place (a short cul-de-sac), about 200 yards past the junction of Clare Road. A footbridge leads to the shed from the end of this cul-de-sac. Walking time 10 minutes.

Cardiff (Canton)

6 May 1962

'1500' 0-6-0PT:	1508

'5700' 0-6-0PT:	3652, 3663, 3748, 3751, 3755, 3784, 4633, 4682, 7749, 8723, 9603, 9630, 9648, 9681, 9713, 9727, 9759, 9761, 9775, 9790, 9794
'2800' 2-8-0:	2889
'4200' 2-8-0T:	4242, 4256, 4270, 5220, 5225, 5230, 5233, 7317
'9700' 0-6-0PT:	8471, 8425, 8466, 8484, 8497, 9437, 9461
'5100' 2-6-2T:	4121, 4169
'4300' 2-6-0:	6330, 6345, 6349, 7307, 7317
'5600' 0-6-2T:	6630
'7400' 0-6-0PT:	7439
'Manor' 4-6-0:	7820 *Dinmore Manor*
'Black 5' 4-6-0:	45021, 45188
'Austerity' 2-8-0:	90125, 90485, 90573, 90579, 90620
'9F' 2-10-0:	92210, 92228, 92232, 92236, 92241
Diesels:	D3260, D7023, D7024, D7029, D7031, D7032

CARLISLE (Canal).

The shed is on the west side of the Hawick line just north of the junction of the Silloth line. The yard is not visible from the line.
Leave Carlisle Station by the main entrance and continue into Court Square. Turn left into English Street, and fork left into Castle Street. Turn left into Annetwell Street, and cross Caldew Bridge. Continue along Bridge Street and Church Street. Fork right into Caldcotes, and continue into Port Road and Newton Road. A broad cinder path leads from the right hand side of this road (opposite Raffles Road) to the shed. Walking time 35 minutes. A bus service labelled Raffles operates between English Street, and the end of Raffles Road.

Carlisle (Canal)

15 August 1954

Class '4' 2-6-0:	43139
'A3' 4-6-2:	60037 *Hyperion*, 60068 *Sir Visto*, 60093 *Coronach*
'V2' 2-6-2:	60840, 60919, 60933
'B1' 4-6-0:	61199, 61217, 61219, 61239, 61395
'K3' 2-6-0:	61854, 61855, 61858, 61882, 61898, 61936, 61937
'D49' 4-4-0:	62732 *Dumfries-shire*
'J35' 0-6-0:	64471, 64499, 64511, 64526
'J39' 0-6-0:	64733, 64877, 64880, 64884, 64888, 64898, 64912, 64930, 64932, 64948, 64964
'J36' 0-6-0:	65216 *Byng*, 65293, 65304, 65312, 65321
'C15' 0-6-0T:	67458, 67474, 67481
'N15' 0-6-2T:	69155, 69174, 69215
'Austerity' 2-8-0:	90539
Diesels:	12084, 12086

KINGMOOR 12A. (Carlisle)
The shed is on the east side of the main line about 1½ miles north of Carlisle Station. The yard is visible from the line.
Leave Carlisle station by the main entrance and go straight ahead into Court Square. Turn left along English Street, and continue into Scotch Street and Rickergate. Cross Eden Bridge and continue up Stanwix Bank. Turn left at the top along Etterby Street and continue along Etterby Scaur. Turn left at the top of the hill into Etterby Road. A broad cinder path leads to the shed from the right hand side of this road (just before the railway bridge). Walking time 45 minutes. A bus service (C3 or C4 St. Anns) runs from English Street to the end of Etterby Road (200 yards from the shed entrance).

Carlisle (Kingmoor)

Wednesday 5 September 1956 (6.55)

'2P' 4-4-0:	40602, 40613, 40615, 40651, 40699
'Crab' 2-6-0:	42720, 42742, 42751, 42803, 42830, 42831, 42837, 42875, 42876, 42884, 42899, 42906, 42914
'3F' 0-6-0:	43241, 43514, 43622
'4F' 0-6-0:	43868, 43902, 32922, 43973, 44008, 44009
'Black 5' 4-6-0:	44675, 44700, 44727, 44792, 44795, 44899, 44902, 44970, 45018, 45083, 45120, 45122, 45138, 45163, 45309, 45330, 45368, 45466, 45481, 45498
'Jubilee' 4-6-0:	45696 Arethusa, 45697 Achilles, 45704 Leviathan, 45729 Furious, 45731 Sanspareil
'Princess Coronation' 4-6-2:	46222 Queen Mary
'3F' 0-6-0T:	45740
'8F' 2-8-0:	48321, 48464, 48616, 48758
'7F' 0-8-0:	49173
'3F' 0-8-0:	56235, 56316, 56332, 56333, 56355, 56373, 56374
'3F' 0-6-0:	57568
'Clan' 4-6-2:	72009 Clan Stewart
Standard '5' 4-6-0:	73003
'Austerity' 2-8-0:	90170, 90628

20 April 1962

Class '4' 2-6-4T:	42233, 42304
'Crab' 2-6-0:	42757, 42801, 42882, 42884, 42901, 42906, 42907
Class '4' 2-6-0:	43027, 43103
'3F' 0-6-0:	43622
'4F' 0-6-0:	43902, 44008, 44009, 44181, 44183, 44277, 44451
'Black 5' 4-6-0:	44666, 44668, 44669, 44673, 44675, 44725, 44878, 44883, 44898, 44899, 44953, 44958, 44969, 44974, 44993, 45072, 45138, 45168, 45334, 45363, 45365, 45457, 45460, 45466, 45481, 45484
'Jubilee' 4-6-0:	45566 Queensland, 45640 Frobisher, 45687 Neptune, 45728 Defiance, 45729 Furious
'Royal Scot' 4-6-0:	46107 Argyll and Sutherland Highlander
'Princess Coronation' 4-6-2:	46224 Princess Alexandra, 46230 Duchess of Buccleuch
Class '2' 2-6-0:	46432
'3F' 0-6-0T:	47332, 47358, 47432, 47471, 47667, 47669
'8F' 2-8-0:	48158, 48758
'3F' 0-6-0:	57568, 57602
'3F' 0-6-0:	57653
'Clan' 4-6-2:	72005 Clan MacGregor, 72006 Clan McKenzie, 72007 Clan Mackintosh, 72008 Clan Macleod, 72009 Clan Stewart
Standard '5' 4-6-0:	73057, 73059, 73154
Standard '4' 2-6-4T:	80020
'Austerity' 2-8-0:	90595, 90763
Diesels:	D59, D63, D91, D138, D3171, D3567 D4107, D8071, D8073

UPPERBY 12B.
The shed is on the east side of the main Penrith line south of Carlisle Station. The yard is visible from the line.
Leave Carlisle Station by the main entrance, and go straight ahead into Court Square. Turn right into Botchergate, and continue into London Road. Turn right into Tyne Street (just past the railway underbridge). This is a short cul-de-sac, and a cinder path leads to the shed from a gate at the end. Walking time 20 minutes.

Carlisle (Upperby)

19 August 1950

'2P' 4-4-0:	40699
Class '4' 2-6-4T:	42601
Stanier 2-6-0:	42984
'4F' 0-6-0:	44081, 44346, 44571
'Black 5' 4-6-0:	44876, 45065, 45083, 45246, 45328, 45409
'Patriot' 4-6-0:	45504 Royal Signals, 45518 Bradshaw, 45525 Colwyn Bay, 45533 Lord Rathmore, 45542
'Jubilee' 4-6-0:	5552 Silver Jubilee, 45586 Mysore, 45737 Atlas
'Royal Scot' 4-6-0:	46157 The Royal Artilleryman
'Princess Coronation' 4-6-2:	46226 Duchess of Norfolk, 46228 Duchess of Rutland
'3F' 0-6-0T:	7221, (4)7295, 47326, (4)7403, 47556, 47666
'8F' 2-8-0:	48263, 48366, 48457

Saturday 30 September 1961

Class '4' 2-6-4T:	42357, 42393, 42571
Class '4' 2-6-0:	43000
'4F' 0-6-0:	44060, 44345, 44346, 44594
'Black 5' 4-6-0:	44834, 44838, 44855, 44939, 45106, 45111, 45185, 45249, 45282, 45293, 45323, 45351, 45371, 45391, 45397, 45408, 45413, 45434, 45440
'Patriot' 4-6-0:	45510 , 45512 Bunsen, 45518 Bradshaw, 45531 Sir Frederick Harrison, 45544
'Jubilee' 4-6-0:	45588 Kashmir, 45632 Tonga, 45652 Hawke, 45728 Defiance
'Princess Coronation' 4-6-2:	46230 Duchess of Buccleuch, 46240 City of Coventry, 46249 City of Sheffield
Class '2' 2-6-0:	46433, 46457, 46458, 46489
'3F' 0-6-0T:	47269, 47288, 47292, 47295, 47326, 47614
'8F' 2-8-0:	48152. 48306, 48433, 48667
'Britannia' 4-6-2:	70017 Arrow, 70046 Anzac

CREWE SOUTH 5B.
The shed is in the fork of the main and Shrewsbury lines south of the station. The yard is partially visible from both lines.
Turn left outside the main entrance to the station. Turn first left into Gresty Road and continue into Gresty Lane. There is a gate on the left hand side between the two railway over-bridges, and a flight of steps just inside the gate. A cinder path leads from the top of these steps to the shed. Walking time 20 minutes.

Crewe South

15 March 1953

Class '4' 2-6-4T:	42113, 42571, 42617
'Crab' 2-6-0:	42783, 42856, 42920
Stanier 2-6-0:	42956, 42968
'3F' 0-6-0:	43207, 43330
'4F' 0-6-0:	44063, 44450, 44508, 44600
'Black 5' 4-6-0:	44709, 44716, 44832, 44838, 44863, 45002, 45024, 45051, 45067, 45074, 45131, 45163, 45164, 45248, 45294, 45350, 45351, 45392, 45418, 45442, 45448, 45451
'Patriot' 4-6-0:	45505 The Royal Army Ordnance Corps
'Royal Scot' 4-6-0:	46115 Scots Guardsman
Sentinel 0-4-0T:	47183, 47184

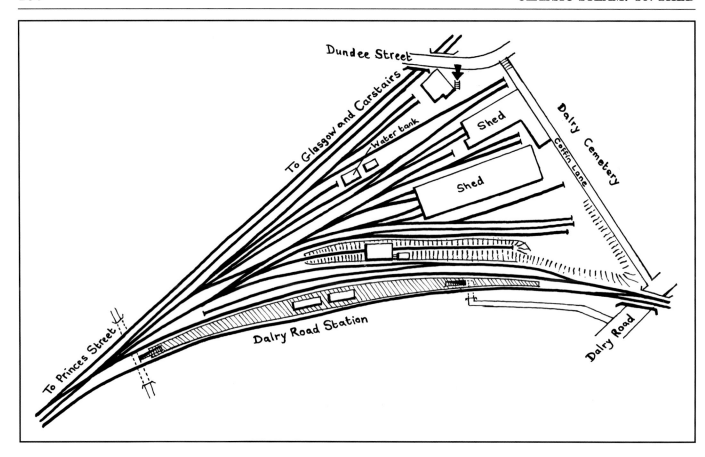

Sketch plan of Dalry Road shed in 1950.

'3F' 0-6-0T:	47266, 47280, 47338, 47384, 47414, 47523, 47524, 47526, 47602, 47616, 47662, 47680
'8F' 2-8-0:	48265, 48288, 48294, 48347, 48470, 48524, 48633, 48725
'7F' 0-8-0:	48952, 49021, 49028, 49157, 49230, 49243, 49311, 49342, 49439
'0F' 0-4-0ST:	51204
'2F' 0-6-0ST:	58221
'Britannia' 4-6-2:	70025 Western Star
Standard '5' 4-6-0:	73024
Standard '4' 4-6-0:	75003, 75010
'Austerity' 2-8-0:	90187, 90563, 90641, 90684, 90720,
Diesels:	12000, 12001, 12002, 12035, 12036, 12050, 12051, 12052, 12053, 12078, 1831

EDINBURGH 28B. (Dalry Road)
The shed is in the fork of the Princes Street-Dalry Road and the Princes Street-Merchiston lines. The yard is visible from the Merchiston line, and partially so from the other line.
Leave Dalry Road Station by the Dalry Road exit. Ascend a flight of steps that lead from Dalry Road to Dundee Street. These steps are on the same side of the road as the station just past the railway bridge. Turn left into Dundee Street, and the shed entrance is on the left hand side just before the railway under-bridge. Walking time 5 minutes.
A tram service labelled 3 Stenhouse or 4 Slateford operates from Princes Street to the bridge by Dalry Road Station.

Dalry Road (Edinburgh)

31 January 1965

'Black 5' 4-6-0:	44820, 45053, 45127, 45469
'B1' 4-6-0:	61245 Murray of Elibank
'J38' 0-6-0:	65912

20 March 1965

Class '4' 2-6-4T:	42283
'Black 5' 4-6-0:	45477, 45483
'B1' 4-6-0:	61134, 61245 Murray of Elibank, 61307
Standard '5' 4-6-0:	73150

2 May 1965

Class '4' 2-6-4T:	42273, 42128
'Black 5' 4-6-0:	44702, 45053, 45359, 45469
'B1' 4-6-0:	61245 Murray of Elibank

DIDCOT.
The shed is on the east side of the Oxford line north of the station. The yard is not visible from the line.
A subway connects the station platforms, and extends to a flight of steps north of the station. A cinder path leads from the top of these steps to the shed. Walking time 5 minutes.

Didcot

22 February 1959

'1400' 0-4-2T:	1407
'2251' 0-6-0:	2214, 2246, 3206, 3210, 3211, 3212, 3219
'2800' 2-8-0:	2819, 2834, 2880, 3818, 3836
'5700' 0-6-0PT:	3622, 3653, 3709, 3721, 3751, 4649, 5737, 5743, 5746, 5783, 5796, 7705
'9400' 0-6-0PT:	9407, 9415, 9417
'4300' 2-6-0:	5324, 5380, 6355 6368, 6370
'5600' 0-6-2T:	5639
'Hall' 4-6-0:	4915 Condover Hall, 4965 Rood Ashton Hall, 4969 Shugborough Hall, 5931 Hatherley Hall, 5932 Haydon Hall, 5936 Oakley Hall, 5954 Faendre Hall, 5981 Harrington Hall, 6906 Chicheley Hall, 6910 Gossington Hall

| 'Modified Hall' 4-6-0: | 6969 *Wraysbury Hall*, 6983 *Otterington Hall*, 6996 *Blackwell Hall* |
| 'Austerity' 2-8-0: | 90152 |

DUNFERMLINE UPPER.

The shed is on the south side of the line east of Dunfermline Upper Station. The yard is visible from the line.

Go straight ahead across the yard outside Dunfermline Upper Station Road. Turn left into James Street, and continue into Holyrood Place. (This road bears left at the traffic roundabout). Turn right along a narrow path that leads from the right hand side of the road between houses Nos. 95 and 97 (just before the railway over-bridge). The shed entrance is on the left hand side of this path. Walking time 10 minutes.

Dunfermline

6 April 1958

'B1' 4-6-0:	61101, 61407
'K2' 2-6-0:	61721, 61738, 61770
'D30' 4-4-0:	62427 *Dumbiedykes*, 62436 *Lord Glenvarloch*, 62441 *Black Duncan*
'J35' 0-6-0:	64476, 64480, 64496, 64513, 64516, 64525
'J37' 0-6-0:	64543, 64568, 64604, 64630
'J36' 0-6-0:	65239, 65253 *Joffre*, 65281, 65320, 65323
'J38' 0-6-0:	65923, 65926, 65928, 65930, 65933
'V3' 2-6-2T:	67669, 67672
'Y9' 0-4-0ST:	68101
'J88' 0-6-0T:	68346, 68350
'N15' 0-6-2T:	69164, 69192, 69202, 69221
'Austerity' 2-8-0:	90547, 90553, 90575, 90600, 90727
Diesels:	11704, 11707, 11718, D3342, 13343, 13344, 13345, 13346

Haymarket (Edinburgh)

Wednesday 12 September 1956, 9.25

'Black 5' 4-6-0:	44954
'A4' 4-6-2:	60004 *William Whitelaw*, 60012 *Commonwealth of Australia*
'A3' 4-6-2:	60037 *Hyperion*, 60043 *Brown Jack*, 60068 *Sir Visto*, 60079 *Bayardo*, 60087 *Blenheim*, 60095 *Flamingo*,

Sketch plan of Haymarket shed in 1960/61.

HAYMARKET.

The shed is on the north side of the line west of the station. The yard is visible from the line.

Turn left outside Haymarket Station into Haymarket Terrace (main road). Continue along West Coates, and turn sharp left into Russell Road. A drive leads to the shed from the right hand side of this road. Walking time 10 minutes.

A tram service labelled Corstorphine (No. 1 or 12) operates between Princess Street (outside Waverley and Princes Street Stations) to the end of Russell Road.

	60097 *Humorist*, 60101 *Cicero*
'V2' 2-6-2:	60816, 60910, 60945, 60951, 60952
'D11' 4-4-0:	62683 *Hobbie Elliott*, 62685 *Malcolm Graeme*, 62691 *Laird of Balmawhapple*, 62693 *Roderick Dhu*
'D49' 4-40:	62704 *Stirlingshire*, 62705 *Lanarkshire*
'J37' 0-6-0:	64820
'J39' 0-6-0:	65258
'J38' 0-6-0:	65914
'V3' 2-6-2T:	67620, 67669
'J83' 0-6-0T:	68457, 68460

LEICESTER 15C.

The shed is on the east side of the main line north of the station. The yard is visible from the line.

Turn left outside Leicester London Road Station into London Road, and first left into Conduit Street. Turn right at the end into Sparkenhoe Street, and left almost immediately into Upper Conduit Street. Fork left into Upper Kent Street, and turn left into Beal Street. The shed entrance is on the left hand side, by the end of this road. Walking time 15 minutes.

Leicester (Midland)

25 August 1963

Class '2' 2-6-2T:	41228, 41279
Class '4' 2-6-4T:	42087, 42184, 42279, 42453
Class '4' 2-6-0:	43012
'4F' 0-6-0:	43988, 44030, 44231, 44284, 44403
'Black 5' 4-6-0:	44804, 44811, 44888, 45040, 45200, 45253, 45267, 45333, 45442
'Jubilee' 4-6-0:	45556 *Nova Scotia*
'8F' 2-8-0:	48119
'B1' 4-6-0:	61249 *FitzHerbert Wright*
Standard '4' 4-6-0:	75051

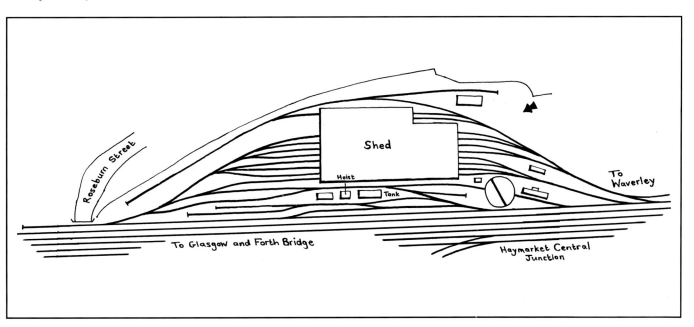

Standard '2' 2-6-2T:	84029
'9F' 2-10-0:	92010, 92070, 92107, 92111, 92112, 92120, 92122, 92123
Diesels:	D3786, D3788, D3789, D3790, D3791, D5814

LOSTOCK HALL 24C.
The shed is at the south side of Lostock Hall Station. The yard is visible from the line.
The shed entrance is a few yards south of the station entrance on the same side of Watkin Lane. Walking time less than 5 minutes.

Lostock Hall

29 January 1956

Class '4' 2-6-4T:	42298, 42421, 42434, 42435, 42481,
'Crab' 2-6-0:	42716, 42723, 42796, 42819
'4F' 0-6-0:	44479
'Black 5' 4-6-0:	44733, 45229, 45363
'2F' 0-6-0ST:	51345, 51423, 51526
'3F' 0-6-0:	52182, 52203, 52290, 52458
'Austerity' 2-8-0:	90314, 90328, 90331, 90335, 90595, 90708

OLD OAK COMMON.
The shed is on the north side of the line east of Old Oak Lane Halt. The yard is not visible from the line.
Turn left outside Willesden (L.M.S. & L.P.T.B.) Station along Old Oak Lane, and turn left again into Old Oak Common Lane. A cinder path leads to the shed from a gate on the left hand side. Walking time 10 minutes.

Old Oak Common

17 April 1954

'County' 4-6-0:	1003 County of Wilts, 1018 County of Leicester, 1019 County of Merioneth
'1500' 0-6-0PT:	1504
'2251' 0-6-0:	2222, 2270, 2282, 2285
'2800' 2-8-0:	2809, 2838, 2844, 3816, 3819, 3857, 3859
'Castle' 4-6-0:	4094 Dynevor Castle, 5014 Goodrich Castle, 5038 Morlais Castle, 5040 Stokesay Castle, 5066 Sir Felix Pole, 5067 St Fagans Castle, 5076 Gladiator, 5093 Upton Castle, 5099 Compton Castle, 7002 Devizes Castle, 7014 Caerhays Castle
'5700' 0-6-0PT:	4673, 7734, 8754, 8757, 8760, 8764, 8767, 8768, 8769, 8771, 8772, 9658, 9700, 9701, 9703, 9704, 9705, 9706, 9707, 9708, 9709, 9725, 9758
'4700' 2-8-0:	4700, 4701, 4702, 4704, 4705, 4707, 4708
'Hall' 4-6-0:	4916 Crumlin Hall, 4931 Hanbury Hall, 4945 Milligan Hall, 4962 Ragley Hall, 4980 Wrottesley Hall, 4986 Aston Hall, 5918 Walton Hall, 5932 Haydon Hall, 5934 Kneller Hall, 5939 Tangley Hall, 5941 Campion Hall, 5975 Winslow Hall, 5982 Harrington Hall, 5986 Arbury Hall, 5996 Mytton Hall
'4300' 2-6-0:	5361, 6387
'6100' 2-6-2T:	6109, 6110, 6130, 6137, 6144, 6158, 6159, 6168
'Grange' 4-6-0:	6807 Birchwood Grange, 6850 Cleave Grange, 6867 Peterston Grange
'Modified Hall' 4-6-0:	6961 Stedham Hall, 6973 Bricklehampton Hall, 7904 Fountains Hall, 7920 Coney Hall, 7925 Westol Hall
'7200' 2-8-2T:	7239
'9400' 0-6-0PT:	8433, 9411, 9418
'Britannia' 4-6-2:	70017 Arrow, 70024 Vulcan
Standard '5' 4-6-0:	73032
Diesel:	13031, 15104, 18000

23 July 1962

| 'County' 4-6-0: | 1007 County of Brecknock, 1009 County of Carmarthen, 1007 County of Caernarvon |

'1500' 0-6-0PT:	1500, 1503, 1504, 1506
'5700' 0-6-0PT:	3754, 8757, 8761, 8771, 9658, 9704, 9706, 9707, 9709, 9710, 9784
'4700' 2-8-0:	4701, 4707, 4708
'Hall' 4-6-0:	4914 Cranmore Hall, 4951 Pendeford Hall, 4970 Sketty Hall, 4982 Acton Hall, 4983 Albert Hall, 5904 Kelham Hall, 5923 Colston Hall, 5932 Haydon Hall, 5964 Wolseley Hall, 5967 Bickmarsh Hall, 5979 Cruckton Hall, 5982 Harrington Hall, 6911 Holker Hall, 6920 Barningham Hall, 6936 Breccles Hall, 6942 Eshton Hall
'Castle' 4-6-0:	5014 Goodrich Castle, 5015 Kingswear Castle, 5032 Usk Castle, 5035 Coity Castle, 5041 Tiverton Castle, 5046 Earl Cawdor, 5052 Earl of Radnor, 5055 Earl of Eldon, 5060 Earl of Berkeley, 5066 Sir Felix Pole, 5068 Beverston Castle, 5080 Defiant, 5082 Swordfish, 5084 Reading Abbey, 5088 Llanthony Abbey, 7008 Swansea Castle, 7017 G. J. Churchward, 7020 Gloucester Castle, 7032 Denbigh Castle
'King' 4-6-0:	6000 King George V, 6009 King Charles II, 6010 King Charles I, 6016 King Edward V, 6021 King Richard II, 6025 King Henry III, 6026 King John, 6028 King George VI, 6029 King Edward VIII
'6100' 2-6-2T:	6125, 6141, 6169
'Modified Hall' 4-6-0:	6961 Stedham Hall, 6962 Soughton Hall, 6973 Bricklehampton Hall, 6989 Wightwick Hall, 6998 Burton Agnes Hall, 7904 Fountains Hall, 7906 Fron Hall, 7909 Heveningham Hall
'9400' 0-6-0PT:	8420, 8458, 9407, 9410, 9420
Standard '4' 2-6-4T:	80069, 80072, 80080, 80096, 80100, 80131, 80134
'9F' 2-10-0:	92203, 92217, 92226
Diesels:	D838 Rapid, D3031, D4000, D7024, D7035

PENZANCE.
The shed is on the north side of the line mid-way between Marizion and Penzance Stations. The yard is visible from the line.
Turn sharp right outside Penzance Station along the main road to the east (A30). The shed entrance is on the right-hand side. Walking time 15 minutes.

Penzance

15 April 1962

'County' 4-6-0:	1004 County of Somerset, 1008 County of Cardigan
'5700' 0-6-0PT:	3635, 9748
'4500' 2-6-2T:	4564, 4670, 5508, 5537, 5562
'Castle' 4-6-0:	5003 Lulworth Castle
'Grange' 4-6-0:	6800 Arlington Grange, 6808 Beanham Grange, 6814 Enborne Grange, 6824 Ashley Grange, 6826 Nannerth Grange, 6833 Calcot Grange, 6835 Eastham Grange, 6868 Penrhos Grange
'9400' 0-6-0PT:	9475
Diesels:	D808 Centaur, D815 Druid, D822 Hercules, D849 Superb, D852 Tenacious, D859 Vanquisher, D6309, D6338

PERTH.
The shed is on the west side of the line just south of Perth General Station. The yard is visible from the line.
Leave Perth General Station by means of the flight of steps that connects the south end of the main platform with the centre of the road over-bridge. Turn right over the bridge, first left into Priory Place, and first left again into a very rough road. The shed entrance is at the end of this road. Walking time less than 5 minutes.

Perth

5 June 1960

| Class '4' 2-6-0: | 43135 |
| '4F' 0-6-0: | 44253, 44258, 44314, 44328 |

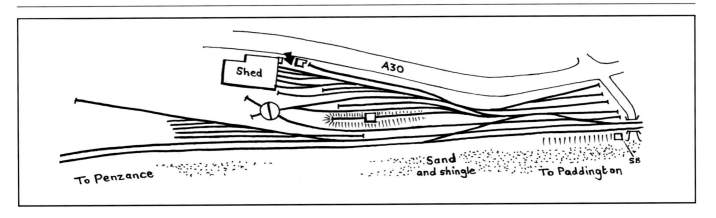

Sketch plans of Penzance shed in 1936 (above), and Perth shed in 1965 (below).

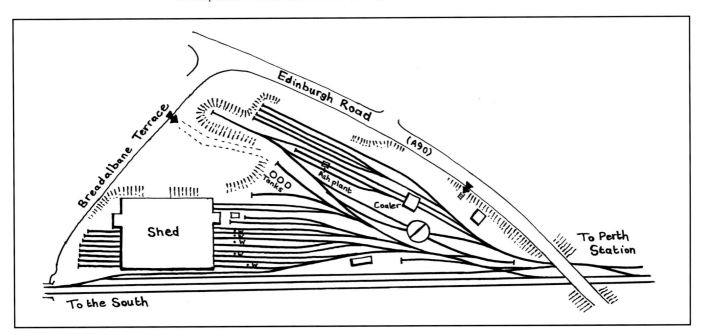

'Black 5' 4-6-0:	44704, 44705, 44801, 44878, 44931, 44980, 44999, 45007, 45016, 45047, 45125, 45158 *Glasgow Yeomanry*, 45165, 45170, 45177, 45309, 45472,, 45481, 45483, 45483, 45496
'Jubilee' 4-6-0:	45657 *Tyrwhitt*
'Princess Coronation' 4-6-2:	46228 *Duchess of Rutland*, 46243 *City of Lancaster*
'3P' 4-4-0:	54485, 54486
'2P' 0-4-4T:	55173, 55200, 55208, 55215
'3F' 0-6-0T:	56246
'2F' 0-6-0:	57257, 57345, 57441, 57473
'3F' 0-6-0:	57554, 57667, 57679
'A2/1' 4-6-2:	60510 *Robert the Bruce*
'V2' 2-6-2:	60822, 60824, 60898
'K2' 2-6-0:	61788 *Loch Rannoch*, 61794 *Loch Oich*
'J35' 0-6-0:	64480
'J37' 0-6-0:	64592, 64624
'Clan' 4-6-2:	72008 *Clan Macleod*
Standard '5' 4-6-0:	73006, 73007, 73008, 73009, 73120, 73146
Standard '4' 2-6-4T:	80093
Diesels:	D1 *Scafell Pike*, D3535, D3541, D3544, D3545, D5116, D5335, D5340, D6145

21 May 1961, 18.45

4F 0-6-0:	44254, 44257, 44314, 44328
'Black 5' 4-6-0:	44698, 44699, 44704, 44720, 44721, 44722, 44796, 44797, 44799, 44801, 44879, 44921, 44925, 44960, 44978, 44979, 44999, 45133, 45361, 45365, 45463,

	45466, 45475, 45476, 45487, 45492
'Princess Coronation' 4-6-2:	46231 *Duchess of Atholl*, 46237 *City of Bristol*, 46244 *King George VI*, 46252 *City of Leicester*
Class '2' 2-6-0:	46468
'3P' 4-4-0:	54486, 54500
'2P' 0-4-4T:	55173, 55217, 55233
'3F' 0-6-0:	56347
'2F' 0-6-0:	57441
'3F' 0-6-0:	57667, 57679
'V2' 2-6-2:	60888, 60959, 60970, 60973
'B1' 4-6-0:	61134
'D11' 4-4-0:	62671 *Bailie MacWheeble*
'J37' 0-6-0:	64617
'J38' 0-6-0:	65912
Standard '5' 4-6-0:	73008, 73079, 73106, 73107, 73120
Standard '4' 2-6-4T:	80126
Diesels:	D335, D3535, D3541, D3542, D3543, D3544, D3545, D5118, D5132, D5325, D5328, D5331, D5337, D5340, D5346, D6120, D6122, D6124, D6128

17 May 1965

'Black 5' 4-6-0:	44703, 44705, 44720, 44881, 44931, 45012, 45043, 45047, 45084, 45319
'B1' 4-6-0:	61180
'Britannia' 4-6-2:	70006 *Robert Burns*, 70036 *Boadicea*
Standard '5' 4-6-0:	73101
Standard '4' 2-6-0:	76103

Standard '2' 2-6-0:	78047
Diesels:	D215 *Aquitania*, D260, D266, D281, D359, D362, D366, D1633, D2717, D3541, D5115, D5304, D5308, D5319, D5333, D5335, D5339, D5341, D5340, D5344

LAIRA.

The shed is on the south side of the main line about two miles east of Plymouth North Road Station. The yard is visible from the line.

Turn right outside Plymouth North Road Station along the approach road, and turn left into St. George's Street. Turn left into North Road and left into Tavistock Road. Continue along Alexandra Road, and Laira Old Road. After a considerable distance, turn right into Brandon Road. This is a cul-de-sac and a footpath leads from the end under the railway, past Laira Halt (closed) to the shed. **Walking time 50 minutes.**

A 'bus service operates between North Road and the end of Brandon Road.

Plymouth (Laira)

15 April 1962

'County' 4-6-0:	1001 *County of Bucks*, 1003 *County of Wilts*
'1361' 0-6-0ST:	1363
'2800' 2-8-0:	2875, 3862
'Castle' 4-6-0:	4087 *Cardigan Castle*, 4095 *Harlech Castle*, 5029 *Nunney Castle*, 5094 *Tretower Castle*
'4500' 2-6-2T:	4555, 4561, 4566, 4567, 4588, 5521, 5532, 5541, 5544, 5564, 5568, 5569, 5572
'5700' 0-6-0PT:	4658, 6771
'Hall' 4-6-0:	4918 *Dartington Hall*, 4982 *Acton Hall*, 5917 *Westminster Hall*, 6938 *Corndean Hall*
'Grange' 4-6-0:	6812 *Chesford Grange*, 6815 *Frilford Grange*, 6825 *Llanvair Grange*, 6831 *Bearley Grange*, 6860 *Aberporth Grange*, 6864 *Dymock Grange*, 6873 *Caradoc Grange*, 6875 *Hindford Grange*
'Modified Hall' 4-6-0:	6988 *Swithland Hall*, 7901 *Dodington Hall*
'7200' 2-8-2T:	7201
'9400' 0-6-0PT:	9467
Class '2' 2-6-2T:	41214
'Warship' A1A-A1A:	D601 *Ark Royal*, D603 *Conquest*
'Warship' B-B:	D804 *Avenger*, D811 *Daring*, D816 *Eclipse*, D821 *Greyhound*, D833 *Panther*, D839 *Relentless*, D841 *Roebuck*, D842 *Royal Oak*, D843 *Sharpshooter*, D850 *Swift*, D853 *Thruster*, D854 *Tiger*, D863 *Warrior*, D868 *Zephyr*, D870 *Zulu*
Other diesels:	D2127, D2175, D2183, D3520, D6300, D6302,

D6303, D6308, D6312, D6313, D6315, D6322, D6329, D6330, D6337

POLMADIE 27A.

The shed is on the east side of the main line south of Eglington Street Station. The yard is partially visible from the line.

Turn right outside the main entrance to Glasgow Central Station along Gordon Street. Turn first right into Union Street and left into Argyle Street. Continue into Trongate, and turn right into Saltmarket. Continue over Albert Bridge into Crown Street. Fork left into Rutherglen Road. Fork left into Rutherglen Road into Polmadie Road (after a considerable distance). The shed entrance is on the left hand side, just before the railway under-bridge. Walking time 40 minutes.

Note: Loco's are sometimes left in a siding on the opposite side of Polmadie Road to the shed.

Polmadie (Glasgow)

6 June 1960

Class '4' 2-6-4T:	42057, 42060, 42143, 42144, 42245, 42265, 42695
'Crab' 2-6-0:	42757, 42835, 42837, 42850
Fowler 4F 0-6-0:	43848, 43849, 43884, 44283
'Black 5' 4-6-0:	44795, 45098, 45172, 45320, 45459
'Patriot' 4-6-0:	45525 *Colwyn Bay*, 45529 *Stephenson*, 45551
'Jubilee' 4-6-0:	45717 *Dauntless*, 45730 *Ocean*, 45731 *Perseverance*, 45742 *Connaught*
'Royal Scot' 4-6-0:	46104 *Scottish Borderer*, 46105 *Cameron Highlander*, 46121 *Highland Light Infantry, City of Glasgow Regiment*
'Princess Royal' 4-6-2:	46206 *Princess Marie Louise*, 46210 *Lady Patricia*
'Princess Coronation' 4-6-2:	46224 *Princess Alexandra*, 46227 *Duchess of Devonshire*, 46230 *Duchess of Buccleuch*
'8F' 2-8-0:	48773, 48774, 48775
'2P' 0-4-4T:	55167, 55169, 55201, 55207, 55220, 55223, 55228, 55237
'2P' 0-4-4T (post-1923):	55265, 55267, 55268
'3F' 0-6-0T:	56239, 56260, 56289, 56292, 56324
'2F' 0-6-0:	57239, 57244, 57250, 57288, 57319, 57365, 57367, 57369, 57389, 57417, 57418, 57432, 57463
'3F' 0-6-0:	57563, 57564, 57581, 57632
'Britannia' 4-6-2:	70051 *Firth of Forth*
'Clan' 4-6-2:	72000 *Clan Buchanan*, 72002 *Clan Campbell*, 72004 *Clan Macdonald*

Sketch plan of Polmadie shed in 1967.

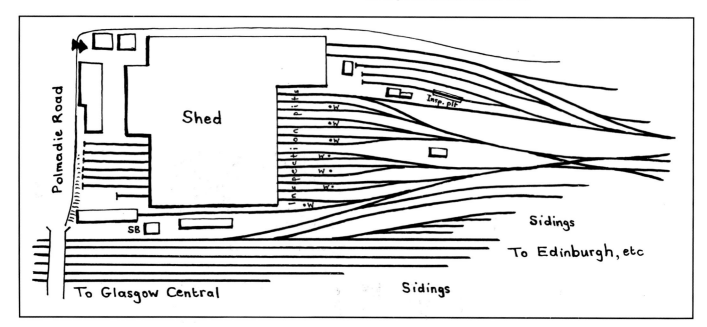

Standard '5' 4-6-0:	73057, 73059, 73060, 73061, 73062, 73064, 73072, 73098
Standard '3' 2-6-0:	77007, 77009
Standard '4' 2-6-4T:	80001, 80002, 80003, 80022, 80056, 80056, 80058, 80106, 80110, 80130
'Austerity' 2-8-0:	90004, 90060, 90229, 90387, 90493, 90536, 90640, 90690, 90705
'Austerity' 2-10-0:	90758, 90767
Diesels:	D3197, D3198, D3383

10 June 1962

Class '4' 2-6-4T:	42055, 42056, 42057, 42058, 42059, 42143, 42144, 42171, 42216, 42243, 42244, 42263, 42265, 42268, 42274, 42276, 42277, 42691
'Crab' 2-6-0:	42850, 42883
'4F' 0-6-0:	44011, 44251, 44283, 44318
'Black 5' 4-6-0:	44719, 44783, 44790, 44885, 44898, 44900, 44973, 44974, 45083, 45151, 45172, 45243, 45458, 45459, 45465, 45478
'Jubilee' 4-6-0:	45583 Assam, 45698 Mars, 45719 Glorious, 45723 Fearless
'Royal Scot' 4-6-0:	46102 Black Watch, 46104 Scottish Borderer, 46114 Coldstream Guardsman, 46121 Highland Light Infantry, City of Glasgow Regiment, 46139 The Welch Regiment
'Princess Royal' 4-6-2:	46203 Princess Margaret Rose
'Princess Coronation' 4-6-2:	46221 Queen Elizabeth, 46223 Princess Alice, 46224 Princess Alexandra, 46231 Duchess of Atholl
'8F' 2-8-0:	48773, 48775, 48774
'3P' 4-4-0:	54463, 54465, 54502
'2F' 0-6-0:	57296, 57360
'3F' 0-6-0:	57555, 57581, 57620, 57622, 57625
'3F' 0-6-0:	57667, 57672, 57674, 57684
'Britannia' 4-6-2:	70023 Venus
'Clan' 4-6-2:	72000 Clan Buchanan, 72001 Clan Cameron, 72002 Clan Campbell, 72003 Clan Fraser
Standard '5' 4-6-0:	73056, 73060, 73063, 73075, 73076, 73098
Standard '3' 2-6-0:	77007, 77008, 77009
Standard '4' 2-6-4T :	80003, 80005, 80026, 80027, 80055, 80056, 80086, 80106, 80107, 80108, 80110, 80112, 80115, 80124, 80129, 80130
'Austerity' 2-8-0:	90039, 90234, 90326, 90387, 90596, 90640
Diesels:	D114, D152, D276, D311, D322, D324, D331, D341, D2431, D2432, D2433, D3199, D3383, D3529, D3906, D3908, D3910, D3911, D3913, D3916, D3917, D3918, D5093, D8086, D8119, D8120, D8124

8 April 1965

Class '4' 2-6-4T:	42131, 42176, 42195, 42197, 42199, 42260
'Black 5' 4-6-0:	44669, 44692, 44721, 44796, 44890, 44953, 45118, 45126
'A2' 4-6-2:	60512 Steady Aim, 60522 Straight Deal, 60524 Herring-bone, 60527 Sun Chariot, 60535 Hornet's Beauty
'Britannia' 4-6-2:	70038 Robin Hood
Standard '5' 4-6-0:	73059, 73062, 73072, 73075, 73098, 73099
Standard '4' 2-6-0:	76070
Standard '4' 2-6-4T:	80060, 80108, 80110, 80120, 80130
Diesels:	D212 Aureol, D215 Aquitania, D232 Empress of Canada, D302, D318, D375, D1633, D2432, D2433, D3200, D3411, D3906, D3907, D3909, D3915, D5017, D5266, D6129, D6134, D8115, D8116, D8117, D8119, D8122, D8123, D8124, D8514, D8518, D8520, D8525, D8526, D8528, D8530, D8531, D8536, D8537, D8541, D8542, D8545, D8551, D8553

Radstock (Dr Cartmel's observations)

7 September 1956

Sentinel 0-4-0T:	47190
'3F' 0-6-0T:	47316, 47542

27 August 1958

Sentinel 0-4-0T:	47191
'3F' 0-6-0T:	47316, 47465, 47496

ST. MARGARETS.

The shed is on both sides of the line about 1¼ miles east of Waverley Station. The yard is visible from the line.

Turn right outside Edinburgh Waverley Station along Princes Street. Continue along Waterloo Place, Regent Road, Montrose Terrace, and London Road. Turn left into Clockmill Road, and the shed entrance is on the right hand side. Walking time 30 minutes.

Tram No. 4 (Piershill) operates from Princes Street, and No. 20 (Joppa), 21 (Leavenhall), 22 (Musselburgh) from Waterloo Place past Clockmill Road.

Note. The office is on the north side of the line by a roundhouse, but the main shed is on the opposite side of the line. Locos may also be left in a small carriage shed, in a siding at the back of the main shed and in a siding on the opposite side of the main road bridge. Owing to the congestion at week-ends a number of small locos are also left at North Leith, South Leith, Granton and other points

Great care should be taken to obey the warning signals when using the boarded crossing over the main line from the roundhouse to the main shed building.

St Margarets (Edinburgh)

Wednesday 12 August 1959

'Black 5' 4-6-0:	45462
Class '2' 2-6-0:	46462
'V2' 2-6-2:	60812, 60813, 60819, 60823, 60846, 60892, 60900, 60901, 60931, 60932, 60933, 60953, 60958, 60971
'B1' 4-6-0:	61191, 61238, 61246, 61308, 61351, 61354, 61359, 61402
'K3' 2-6-0:	61818, 61858, 61878, 61881, 61909, 61916, 61924, 61968, 61992
'D34' 4-4-0:	62487 Glen Arklet
'D49' 4-4-0:	62711 Dumbartonshire, 62718 Kinross-shire
'J35' 0-6-0:	64482, 64483, 64506, 64515
'J37' 0-6-0:	64538, 64547, 64572, 64603, 64608, 64611, 64613, 64624
'J36' 0-6-0:	65259
'J38' 0-6-0:	65914, 65915, 65916, 65918, 65919, 65929, 65934
'V1/3' 2-6-2T:	67606, 67649, 67659, 67666, 67670
'Y9' 0-4-0ST:	68095, 68104
'J83' 0-6-0:	68472, 68477
'N15' 0-6-2T:	69149, 69150, 69173, 69185, 69186

11 February 1961

'Jubilee' 4-6-0:	45715 Invincible
'A3' 4-6-2:	60037 Hyperion, 60090 Grand Parade,
'V2' 2-6-2:	60816, 60818, 60824, 60868, 60873 Coldstreamer, 60882, 60910, 60953, 60965, 60973
'B1' 4-6-0:	61029 Chamois, 61064, 61099, 61219, 61307, 61341, 61357
'D49' 4-4-0:	62718 Kinross-shire, 62729 Rutlandshire, 62744 The Holderness
'J35' 0-6-0:	64519, 64524
'J37' 0-6-0:	64547, 64553, 64557, 64566, 64576, 64590, 64599, 64614, 64637
'J36' 0-6-0:	65329
'J38' 0-6-0:	65906, 65916, 65927
'V2/3' 2-6-2T:	67615, 67649
'Y9' 0-4-0ST:	68095
'J88' 0-6-0T:	68342
'J83' 0-6-0T:	68453, 68470, 68477
'N15' 0-6-2T:	69134
Standard '5' 4-6-0:	73078
'Austerity' 2-8-0:	90149
Diesels:	D250, D278, D2747, D2750, D2751, D2754, D3732, D3733, D3734, D3736, D3742, D3883, D3885, D3886, D3889, D3893

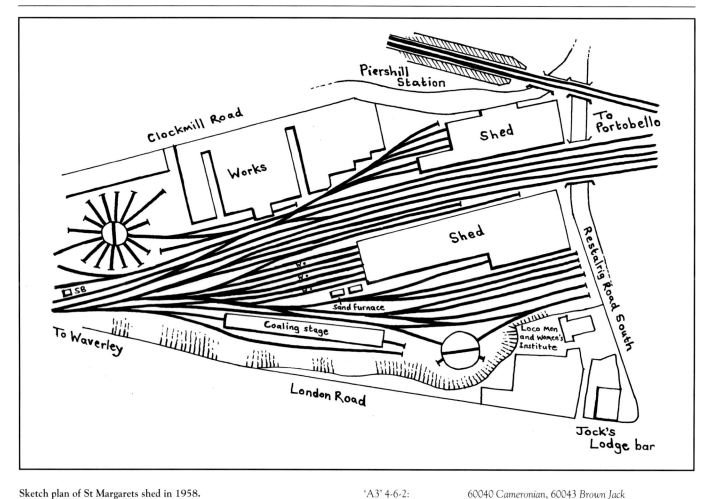

Sketch plan of St Margarets shed in 1958.

24 August 1962

'Black 5' 4-6-0:	45161, 45178
Class '2' 2-6-0:	46462
'A4' 4-6-2:	60001 *Sir Ronald Matthews*
'A3' 4-6-2:	60041 *Salmon Trout*, 60043 *Brown Jack*, 60071 *Tranquil*, 60072 *Sunstar*, 60087 *Blenheim*
'A2' 4-6-2:	60534 *Irish Elegance*, 60537 *Bachelor's Button*, 60538 *Velocity*
'V2' 2-6-2:	60813, 60816, 60836, 60840, 60873 *Coldstreamer*, 60883, 60892, 60894, 60910, 60931, 60933, 60937, 60951, 60965, 60969, 60971, 60973
'B1' 4-6-0:	61007 *Klipspringer*, 61108, 61117, 61294, 61307, 61341, 61344, 61349, 61350, 61356, 61357, 61398
'K3' 2-6-0:	61968
'J35' 0-6-0:	64510, 64519, 64527
'J37' 0-6-0:	64547, 64557, 64562, 64572, 64576, 64577, 64582, 64591, 64594, 64606, 64607, 64608, 64637
'J36' 0-6-0:	65224 *Mons*, 65344
'J38' 0-6-0:	65914, 65918, 65920, 65927, 65934
'V1/3' 2-6-2T:	67668
'Y9' 0-4-0 ST:	68095
'J83' 0-6-0T:	68477
'N15' 0-6-2T:	69219
Standard '4' 2-6-4T:	80003, 80022, 80026, 80055
Diesels:	D2706, D2720, D2722, D2728, D2729, D2731, D2745, D2779, D3558, D3742, D3878, D3880, D3886

9 May 1964

Class '4' 2-6-4T:	42128, 42163, 42239, 42691
'Black 5' 4-6-0:	45327
Class '2' 2-6-0:	46462

'A3' 4-6-2:	60040 *Cameronian*, 60043 *Brown Jack*
'A1' 4-6-2:	60116 *Hal o' the Wynd*, 60127 *Wilson Worsdell*
'V2' 2-6-2:	60824, 60882, 60931
'B1' 4-6-0:	61118, 61147, 61244 *Strang Steel*, 61324, 61357, 61398, 61404
'J37' 0-6-0:	64572, 64591
'J38' 0-6-0:	65914, 65920, 65922, 65927
'N15' 0-6-2T:	69128
Standard '4' 2-6-4T:	80006, 80026, 80054, 80114, 80122
Diesels:	D262, D275, D368, D2705, D2715, D2720, D2722, D2723, D2724, D2728, D2731, D2748, D2749, D3732, D3878, D3882, D3887, D3892, D3893, D8561, D8563, D8565, D8569, D8577, D8579

14 February 1965

'Black 5' 4-6-0:	44672, 45138
'A4' 4-6-2:	60024 *Kingfisher*, 60027 *Merlin*
'A3' 4-6-2:	60052 *Prince Palatine*, 60100 *Spearmint*
'V2' 2-6-2:	60824, 60955, 60957, 60970
'B1' 4-6-0:	61191, 61345, 61349, 61350, 61357
'J38' 0-6-0:	65915
Standard '4' 2-6-4T:	80022, 80114, 80122
Diesels:	D181, D190, D270, D361, D338, D1525

TEMPLECOMBE 22D.
    The shed is on the east side of the S. & D. line north of the point where it goes under the main S.R. line. The yard is visible from the S. & D. line.
    Turn left outside the S.R. Station along the approach road. Turn left under the railway bridge, and first right over the S. & D. line. A broad path leads to the shed from the left hand side of this road. Walking time 10 minutes.

WILLESDEN 1A.
    The shed is on the west side of the main line just north of the station. The yard is partially visible from the line.
    Turn left outside Willesden (L.M.S. or L.P.T.B.) Station along Old Oak Lane, and take the first turning on the right. This is a short cul-de-sac, and a path leads from the end to the shed. Walking time 5 minutes.

Templecombe (Dr Cartmel's observations)

10 September 1953

'2P' 4-4-0:	40505, 40509, 40564, 40601, 40698
Class '2' 2-6-2T:	41248
'3F' 0-6-0:	43201, 43248, 43436
'4F' 0-6-0:	44102, 44557, 44561
'Black 5' 4-6-0:	44839 (71G)
'7F' 2-8-0:	53807

Sunday 2 September 1956, 5 pm

'G6' 0-6-0T:	30274
'Z' 0-8-0T:	30953
'2P' 4-4-0:	40563, 40564, 40568, 40569, 40601 (71G)
Class '2' 2-6-2T:	41249
'3F' 0-6-0:	43194, 43216, 43218, 43248, 43356, 43419
'4F' 0-6-0:	44102, 44557
'7F' 2-8-0:	53803 (71G), 53808 (71G)
Standard '4' 4-6-0:	75071 (71G)

Saturday 9 April 1960

'2251' 0-6-0:	3218 (82G)
'2P' 4-4-0:	40537, 40564, 40634, 40652 (82G)
'3F' 0-6-0:	43194 (82G), 43218, 43436
'4F' 0-6-0:	44523, 44561 (82F)
'3F' 0-6-0T:	47542
'7F' 2-8-0:	53803
Standard '5' 4-6-0:	73049 (82F), 73052
Standard '4' 4-6-0:	75027 (82G)

13 July 1960, 6.30 pm

'5700' 0-6-0PT:	3720 (82G)
'2P' 4-4-0:	40537, 40563 (82G), 40569 (82G), 40700 (82F)
Class '2' 2-6-2T:	41248 (82G)
'3F' 0-6-0:	43216 (82G), 43427 (82G)
'4'F 0-6-0:	44102, 44417 (82G)
Standard '5' 4-6-0:	73047

Willesden

17 April 1954

Class '3' 2-6-2T:	40004, 40016, 40018, 40042, 40046, 40047, 40049, 40051, 40052, 40054, 40055, 40066, 40069

'2P' 4-4-0:	40529
Class '4' 2-6-4T:	42061, 42062, 42118
'Crab' 2-6-0:	42747, 42870, 42885, 42931, 42933, 42937, 42966, 42979
'4F' 0-6-0:	44116, 44364, 44372, 44397, 44442, 44451, 44497
'Black 5' 4-6-0:	44715, 44838, 44865, 44870, 44875, 44915, 44916, 45005, 45025, 45027, 45089, 45094, 45249, 45308, 45374
'Patriot' 4-6-0:	45511 *Isle of Man*, 45517, 45546 *Fleetwood*
'Jubilee' 4-6-0:	45591 *Udaipur*, 45592 *Indore*
Class '2' 2-6-0:	46431, 46433
'3F' 0-6-0T:	47304, 47361, 47378, 47474, 47475, 47492, 47520, 47675, 47676
'8F' 2-8-0:	48074, 48122, 48134, 48312, 48325, 48366, 48416, 48440, 48476, 48629, 48656, 48675, 48681, 48757
'7F' 0-8-0:	49068, 49139, 49164, 49180, 49227, 49344
Standard '5' 4-6-0:	73041
Diesel:	12021

24 July 62

Fowler 2-6-2T:	40006, 40049
Stanier 2-6-2T:	40080, 40128, 40144, 40157, 40201
Fairburn 2-6-4T:	42101, 42117, 42218, 42234
Fowler 2-6-4T:	42367
Stanier 2-6-4T:	42470, 42478, 42562, 42576, 42577, 42588, 42604, 42611, 42616
Stanier 2-6-0:	42983
'4F' 0-6-0:	44442
'Black 5' 4-6-0:	45048, 45111, 45236, 45255, 45271, 45287, 45 328
'Patriot' 4-6-0:	45523 *Bangor*, 45529 *Stephenson*
'Jubilee' 4-6-0:	45555 *Quebec*, 45655 *Keith*, 45732 *Sanspareil*
'Royal Scot' 4-6-0:	46111 *Royal Fusilier*, 46119 *Lancashire Fusilier*, 46144 *Honorable Artillery Company*, 46146 *The Rifle Brigade*, 46154 *The Hussar*
Class '2' 2-6-0:	46426, 46470
'3F' 0-6-0T:	47302, 47304, 47307
'8F' 2-8-0:	48036, 48325, 48368, 48449, 48518, 48538, 48600, 48601, 48624, 48637, 48751
'7F' 0-8-0:	49413
'Britannia' 4-6-2:	70021 *Morning Star*, 70025 *Western Star*, 70031 *Byron*, 70033 *Charles Dickens*, 70040 *Clive of India*
Standard '5' 4-6-0:	73013, 73014, 73039, 73126
Standard '4' 4-6-0:	75030, 75037, 75038, 75052, 75054
Standard '4' 2-6-0:	76023
'9F' 2-10-0:	92086
Diesels:	D5000, D5001, D5016, D5024, D5029, D5030, D5035, D5073, D5074, D5076, D5082, D5136, D5137, D5141, D5143, D5144, D5145, D5146, D5604, D8003, D8036, D8041, 10000

Bibliography

General

Banks, C. *British Railways Locomotives 1948* (Haynes/Oxford Publishing Co, 1990). Engine depots and codes at 1 January 1948. Locomotive numbers and allocation on that date.

Behrend, G. *Gone With Regret* 3rd ed (Jersey Artists, 1969). A delightfully eccentric book describing many aspects of the Great Western Railway at the height of its influence.

Carter, J. R. *Footplate Cameraman* (Ian Allan Ltd). Album containing very good photographs indeed of locomotives on shed at Edge Hill, Sutton Oak, Crewe North, Patricroft and Chester.

Coleman, R. and Rajczonek, J. *Railway Images around Northamptonshire* (W. D. Wharton, Wellingborough, 1992). Superbly produced album containing a section ('Down by the loco shed') depicting mpds at Banbury, Woodford Halse, Northampton, New England, Wellingborough and Kettering.

Esau, M. (compiler) *John Ashman Rail Portfolio* (Haynes/Oxford Publishing Co, 1988). Among the technically faultless photographs are several of engines on shed, particularly Reading shed in the late 1920s. Powerful studies of locomotives at Stewarts Lane, Camden and King's Cross sheds are superb.

Fish, D. S. *Steam on the South Devon Banks* (South Anglia Productions, Frinton). One of Britain's best railway photographers.

Gifford, C. T. *Decline of Steam* (Ian Allan, 1965). The book that influenced a generation of railway photographers. Inspired shots at Holbeck, Tyseley, Sunderland, Oban, Polmadie, Nine Elms, Three Bridges, Cambridge, etc (at least 46) including the wonderful 'Hot Work', 'Evening at Carlisle (Canal)' and '6842 at Laira'.

Steam Finale North (Ian Allan Ltd, Shepperton, 1976). Some of the shed photographs almost have the same impact as his earlier book. Very good shots in roundhouses at West Hartlepool, Sunderland, York and Neville Hill.

Hands, P. and Richards, C. *British Railways Steaming On The London Midland Region* Vol 1 (Defiant Publications, Shirley, Solihull, 1985). One of a large series of books containing some photographs with considerable potential, possibly under-exploited - 45 plates depicting engines on a large variety of sheds.

British Railways Steaming on the ex-LNER Lines Vol 1 (Defiant Publications, Shirley, Solihull, 1988). Again a mixture of uninspired and interesting shots. Depots depicted include Darnall, Norwich, Peterborough (Spital Bridge), Hull (Botanic Gardens), Dundee (Tay Bridge), 64A and 64B.

British Railways Steaming on the ex-LNER Lines Vol 2 (Defiant Publications, Shirley, Solihull, 1991). Depicts Frodingham, Doncaster, Canklow, Kipps, Seafield, St Boswells and Polmont among many others.

Hodgson, J. T. and Lake, C. S. *Locomotive Management - Cleaning, Driving, Maintenance* 9th edition (The Railway Magazine, 1953). Concerned with the working and maintenance of locomotives and aimed at running shed staff, cleaners, mechanics, enginemen, etc.

Hucknall, D. J. *Twilight of Scottish Steam* (Haynes/Oxford Publishing Co, Sparkford, 1988). Contains many shed photographs, usually in 1964/5, at 63A, 64A, 61B, 62A, 62B and others.

Jenkinson, D. and Whitehouse, P. *Eric Treacy's LMS* (Haynes/Oxford Publishing Co, Sparkford, 1988). Throughout there are fascinating photographs of the depots at Bangor, Camden, Edge Hill, Holyhead, Llandudno Junction and Carlisle Upperby.

Peters, I. *The Somerset and Dorset: An English Cross-country Railway* (Oxford Publishing Co, Oxford, 1974). Photographs showing Bath, Radstock and Templecombe mpds. Many of the shots at Bath are very good.

The Somerset and Dorset in the Fifties, Vol 2 1955-59 (Oxford Publishing Co, Poole, 1981). Photographs of locomotives on shed at Bath.

Whitehouse, P. and Powell, J. *Treacy's Routes North* (Book Club Associates, 1985). This contains a section entitled 'On Shed'. It contains some superbly sharp portrayals of engines. Three of them - 46140 at 8A, 72007 at Kingmoor and a shot of Gateshead shed with 60084 - are especially good.

Reminiscences

In the 1970s D. Bradford Barton Ltd of Truro introduced a series of paperbacks written by footplatemen on aspects of their career. Some were more memorable than others. I have not managed to read every one, but a good proportion are highly readable:

Bushell, G. *LMS Locos from the Footplate*.

Drayton, J. *On the Footplate* (1976). Aspects of shed life at Ebbw Junction, Banbury and Pontypool Road sheds.

Essery T. *Firing Days at Saltley*. In my opinion one of the best of the Bradford Barton series. Describes in excellent detail activities in and around Saltley shed and the work of some of the shed's links.

Fleming, D. J. *St Philip's Marsh - Memories of an Engine Shed*. Well-written. A memorable sentence form it, concerning the shed's final day, is: 'I walked into the coal yard, pulling a few points as I went, just to be able to say that I was the last man to do so.'

Other titles are:

Hardy, R. H. N. *Steam World* No 45, March 1991, p42. Brief indications of life at Stewarts Lane mpd, Battersea.

Higson, M. F. *London Midland Fireman* (Ian Allan Ltd, London, 1976).

Jackman, M. *Engineman SR* (D. Bradford Barton Ltd, Truro).

Jeffryes, A. 'On Shed', *Trains Illustrated*, September 1953, p33. A short article on the activities in and around Holbeck.

Johnson, P. G. *Through the Links at Crewe* (D. Bradford Barton Ltd, Truro). Life at Gresty Lane and Crewe North and South sheds.

Meacher, C. *Living with Locos* (D. Bradford Barton Ltd, Truro).

'Filling in for the "Gaffer"', *Steam World*, September 1991, p23. Article on the duties of the Running Shed Foreman at St Margarets.

Venning, R. 'Southern Evacuee', *Steam World*, No 50, August 1991, p42. A brief article but containing some rather good portraits of engines at various London depots in the mid-1940s.

Motive Power Depots

General

ABC Locoshed Book published at intervals over many years (Ian Allan Ltd). The classic pocket book, containing the allocations of every British Railways locomotive.

Beavor, E. S. *Steam Motive Power Depots* (Ian Allan Ltd, London, 1983).

Ramsey, H. *Capital Steam* (Haynes/Oxford Publishing Co, Sparkford, 1989). An immensely enjoyable book recounting the events of a few days in the school and summer holidays when every shed in the London area (from Stratford to Southall and from Kentish Town to Northwood Junction) was visited. The photographs are also very good.

Sawford, E. 'The Lure of the Loco Shed', *The Railway Magazine* supplement, October 1990.

Smith, P. *The Handbook of Steam Motive Power Depots* Vol 2 Central England, East and Wales (Platform 5 Publications Ltd, Sheffield). One of a series of books which seem neither one thing nor the other. It shows the immediate vicinity around mpds from contemporary Ordnance Survey maps, illustrating them with selected small photographs.

The Handbook of Steam Motive Power Depots Vol 3 North Midlands, Lancashire and Yorkshire (Platform 5 Publications Ltd, Sheffield, 1990).

Whitehouse, P. B. *Steam on Shed* (Ian Allan Ltd, Shepperton, 1969). A book with a promising title and cover. In fact, a tedious mixture of close-ups of locomotives on shed in France, Turkey, Hungary and several other countries, with some uninspiring photographs of British engines.

Eastern/North Eastern Regions

Bolger, P. *BR Steam Motive Power Depots, ER* (Ian Allan Ltd, London 1982).

Hands, P. B. *What Happened to Steam* Vol 13 The LNER B1s (1981). Allocations of all B1s from January 1957 to their disposal.

What Happened to Steam Vol 8 The LNER V2 2-6-2s (1980. Reprinted 1984 and associated volumes).

Hawkins, C. and Reeve, G. *GE Railway Engine Sheds* Part 1 Stratford, Peterborough and Norwich Districts (Wild Swan Publications, Didcot, 1986).

GE Railway Engine Sheds Part 2 Ipswich and

Cambridge Districts (Wild Swan Publications, Didcot, 1987).

Hooper, J. *LNER Sheds in Camera* (Oxford Publishing Co, Poole, 1984). 303 photographs at 125 separate locations.

Preedy, N. E. *North Eastern Pacifics* (D. Bradford Barton Ltd, Truro, 1974). Contains fine portraits of 'A1s', 'A2s', 'A3s' and 'A4s' at Heaton, Haymarket, Dundee, Ferryhill, Gateshead, Doncaster, Darlington and Grantham.

Railway Correspondence and Travel Society, *Locomotives of the LNER*. Various volumes. Immense detail regarding individual locomotives in certain cases, including allocations at selected periods through their lifetimes.

Treacy, E. *Portrait of Steam* (Ian Allan Ltd, London, 1967). Gateshead, York and Grantham. Treacy was one of the few photographers who succeeded in taking good, interesting shots at York.

Wells, J. A. *The Blyth and Tyne Branch 1874-1989, Blyth and Tyne Part II* (Northumberland County Library, Morpeth, 1990). Contains a chapter on the mpds at North and South Blyth and Percy Main and their allocations.

London Midland Region

Bolger, P. *BR Steam Motive Power Depots, LMR* (Ian Allan Ltd, 1981, reprinted 1984).

'45562' (compiler) *London Midland Steam on Shed* (D. Bradford Barton Ltd, Truro, 1978). Plans of - and in most cases portraits of - locomotives in and around depots (43), including 1A, 1B, 1D, 3A, 3C, 5A 5B, 5D and others.

London Midland Steam on Shed 2 (D. Bradford Barton Ltd, Truro). Continuation of above to 1C, 2A, Coventry, Monument Lane, Chester, 8A, Brunswick, Stockport, Edgeley and so on.

Forsythe, H. G. 'Royal Scot disposal' *Trains Illustrated*, October 1960. Photo feature showing the disposal of 46126 at 1B after a trip from Carlisle.

Hands, P. B. *What happened to Steam* The London Midland Patriot, Royal Scot, Princess and Coronation Classes (Hands, 1980, 2nd impression 1981).

Hawkins, C. and Reeve G. *LMS Engine Sheds (Their History and Development)* Vol 1 The LNWR (Wild Swan Publications Ltd, Didcot, 1987). To quote from the Introduction, the series attempts to describe in as much detail as possible those sheds operated by the LMS at the close of its existence in 1947. The first two chapters give good accounts of coaler development, ash handling plants and the LMS's maintenance system.

LMS Engine Sheds (Their History and Development) Vol 2 The Midland Railway (Wild Swan Publications Ltd, Didcot, 1981). A very well produced book, presumably the definitive work, containing excellent track plans and some very good photographs.

LMS Engine Sheds (Their History and Development) Vol 3 The Lancashire and Yorkshire Railway (Wild Swan Publications Ltd, Didcot, 1982).

LMS Engine Sheds (Their History and Development) Vol 4 The Smaller English Constituents (Furness Railway, London, Tilbury and Southend, North Staffordshire Railway, SMJR, S&D) (Wild Swan Publications Ltd, Didcot, 1984).

Hooper, J. *London Midland & Scottish Railway. Locomotive Allocations. The Last Day 1947* (Irwell Press, Pinner, 1989).

Treacy, E. *Portraits of Steam* (Ian Allan Ltd, London, 1967). Some shots of locomotives on shed at Holyhead, Holbeck (including the excellent shot of 46103 and 45704 'Nose to Nose'), Upperby and Camden.

Scottish Region

Bolger, P. *BR Steam Motive Power Depots, Sc R* (Ian Allan Ltd, 1983).

Hawkins, C. and Reeve, G. *LMS Engine Sheds (Their History and Development)* Vol 5 The Caledonian Railway (Wild Swan Publications, Didcot, 1987).

Hay, P. (compiler) *British Railways Steaming through Scotland* (Defiant Publications, Shirley, Solihull, 1991). Very much the mixture as before in all this series.

Morrison, B. *Scottish Steam Album* (Oxford Publishing Co, Oxford, 1978). Contains photo features on 64B, 64A, 62B, 61B, 61A, 60A, 63A, 65B, 65E, 65A, 66D.

Treacy, E. *Portrait of Steam* (Ian Allan Ltd, London 1967). Contains shots of engines at Beattock shed, Haymarket and St Margarets, and Kingmoor.

Southern Region

Armstrong, P. (compiler and publisher) *Southern Region Allocations* (published on behalf of the LCGB). Allocations at 3 March 1953.

Bolger, P. *BR Steam Locomotive Motive Power Depots, SR* (Ian Allan Ltd, London, 1983).

Bradley, D. L. *An Illustrated History of LSWR Locomotives: The Urie Classes* (Wild Swan Publications, Didcot, 1987). Superbly produced and illustrated. Details of the locomotives including their initial allocations.

Locomotives of the Southern Railway Part 2 (Railway Correspondence and Travel Society, London, 1976). An immense amount of detail concerning the 'Merchant Navy', 'West Country' and 'Battle of Britain' Classes, including shed allocations.

Conolly, W. P. *Southern Mainline Cameraman* (ed Esau, M.) (Oxford Publishing Co, Poole, 1986). Includes 24 photographs of engines on shed. Particularly impressive are the studies of No 35009 at 72A and No 30765 at Basingstoke shed. Delightful too is the portrait of 'M7' No 30107 outside Swanage shed on a hot afternoon.

Fairclough, T. and Wills, A. *More Southern Steam on Shed* (D. Bradford Barton Ltd, 1975). Including Bournemouth, Feltham, Fratton, Eastleigh, 72A, 73A, Yeovil, Swanage and others.

Griffiths, R. *Southern Sheds in Camera* (Haynes/Oxford Publishing Co Ltd, 1989). Shed details in alphabetical order.

Hawkins, C. and Reeve, G. *LSWR Engine Sheds, W District* (Irwell Press, Pinner, 1990). Very good account of sheds at Salisbury, Yeovil, Exeter, Barnstaple, Plymouth and Wadebridge.

Treacy, E. *Portrait of Steam* (Ian Allan Ltd, London, 1967). A few shots of the mpds at Nine Elms.

Western Region

Arlett, M. and Lockett, D. *The Norman Lockett Collection - Great Western Steam in the West Country* (Haynes/Oxford Publishing Co, 1990, reprinted 1991). Contains colour photographs at 82A (2) and 83C (2); also two classical black and white studies of 82A with (i) 5040 at the coaler and (ii) 7033/6986/1009 lined up outside.

Bolger, P. *BR Steam Motive Power Depots, WR* (Ian Allan Ltd, 1983). Allocations of steam locomotives in 1950, 1959 and 1965 (if still open) at the major Western Region sheds. One of an excellent series of books.

Copsey, J. 'Cornish "Halls" in the 1930s', *Great Western Journal*, Cornish Special Issue, late summer 1992. Allocations of the '49XX' and '59XX' Classes from 1929 to 1939 given within a detailed article on duties.

Copsey, J. and Clifton, M. 'Banbury - The shed, the engines and the men', *Great Western Journal* No 3, Summer 1992. A very detailed article on Banbury shed from 1950 to 1966. Well illustrated with particularly good plans.

Griffiths, R. *GWR Sheds in Camera* (Haynes/Oxford Publishing Co, 1987, reprinted 1988). The book features some 160 sheds of the former GWR and absorbed companies. A book with many excellent detailed photographs and many 'just for the record' pictures of variable quality.

Hands, P. *BR Steam Shed Allocations Part 1 Western Region Sheds 81A-81F, 82A-82F, 83A-83G* (Defiant Publications, 1985). Lists the individual steam locomotives at the depots of Western Region in the 81-86 Divisions from January 1959 until either complete closure or withdrawal of steam.

Hands, P. and Richard, C. (compiler) *British Railways Steaming on the Western Region*, Vol 1 (Defiant Publications, Shirley, Solihull, 1985). The introduction states that the book and others in the series were 'designed to give the ordinary, everyday photographic enthusiasts . . . a chance to participate in and give pleasure to others whilst recapturing the twilight days of steam'. Sheds illustrated include 81A, 81C, 81D, 81E, 82A, 82B, 82C, 84A, 84B, 84C, 84D, 84E, 84G, 86A, 87E, 87F, 87G.

British Railways Steaming on the Western Region Vol 2 (Defiant Publications, Shirley, Solihull, 1987). Photographs taken at 84E, 84G, 84H, 81A, 81C, 81E, 81F, 82A, 82B, 82C, 82F, 83B, 83C, 83G, 85A, 85B, 86J, 87D, 88B, 89B and Aberbeeg.

Maggs, C. G. *Taunton Steam* (Millstream Books, 1991). Describes in great detail the motive power in and around Taunton from the 1930s to the '60s, including details of the shed links. Loco allocation in 1922, 1947 and 1959.

Williams, C. L. (ed) *Great Western Steam Miscellany* Vol 1 (D. Bradford Barton Ltd, Truro, 1977). Contains a short photographic portrait by C. J. Blay of Reading shed.

Great Western Steam on Shed (D. Bradford Barton Ltd, Truro, 1974). Photographs of 81A, 81B, 81C, 81E, Westbury, 83A, 83C, 83D, 83E, 83F, Tyseley, Stourbridge, etc.

More Great Western Steam on Shed (D. Bradford Barton Ltd, Truro, 1976). A good portrayal of a wide range of engine sheds (81D, 81F, 82A, 82B, 82C, 82F, 83G, 84B, 84C, etc). As with most of the series, most of the photographs are 'workmanlike', others 'merely for the record'.

Index